COPYRIGHT 2024 BY BARBARA GLISSC

All rights reserved. No part of this publication may be reproduced, transmitted in any form or by any means, including photocopying, recording, or other electronic or mechanical methods, without the prior written permission of the publisher, except in the case of brief quotations embodied in critical reviews and specific other non-commercial purposes permitted by copyright law.

DISCLAIMER

The information provided in this cookbook is for informational and educational purposes only. It should not be construed as professional medical advice or a substitute for consultation with a healthcare professional. Before initiating any dietary changes, consult your physician or qualified healthcare provider. The author and publisher are not responsible for any adverse effects or consequences resulting from the use of recipes, suggestions, or procedures described in this book. Use your own discretion when following the recipes in this book.

CONTENTS

INTRODUCTION 2

CHAPTER 1: OVERVIEW AND PRINCIPLES OF THE CARNIVORE DIET 3
1.1 What are the main benefits of the carnivore diet? 4
1.2 Who may need a carnivore diet? 5
1.3 Common Misconceptions About the Carnivore Diet 5

CHAPTER 2: BEGINNING A CARNIVORE DIET 7
2.1 Three critical steps to switch to a carnivore diet... 7
2.2 Understand the physical and psychological changes you may experience during transition 8
2.3 Effective tips will help maintain nutritional balance and long-term adherence to the diet 9
2.4 Safety considerations and health effects 10

CHAPTER 3: PERMITTED AND PROHIBITED PRODUCTS 11
3.1 Allowed products... 11
3.2 Foods that should be excluded from the diet 12

CHAPTER 4: USING AN AIR FRYER ON A CARNIVORE DIET 13
4.1 Benefits of using an air fryer in a Carnivore diet 14
4.2 Air fryer maintenance and safety tips 15
4.3 Temperature and Time Guide for Air Frying Meat 17

CHAPTER 5: TYPES OF STEAKS AND THEIR PREPARATION 18
5.1 An overview of the different types of steak, with tips for selecting and preparing each cut for optimal flavor and nutritional value 18
5.2 The importance of grass-fed meat 19
5.3 Benefits of wild fish 20

CHAPTER 6: WHAT IMPORTANT VITAMINS ARE PRESENT IN MEAT 22

CHAPTER 7: PROBLEMS THAT MAY ARISE AND THEIR SOLUTIONS 24
7.1 How to deal with carbohydrate and sugar cravings: effective strategies ... 26
7.2 Identifying and preventing nutritional deficiencies...................................... 27
7.3 Long-term strategies for diet maintenance and transition......................... 28

CHAPTER 8: BREAKFAST RECIPES 29

1. Bacon and Eggs 30	10. Shrimp and Egg Scramble 34
2. Pork Sausage................................ 30	11. Cod and Egg Breakfast Bowls 35
3. Beef Steak and Eggs 31	12. Bacon and Steak Frittata 35
4. Ham and Egg Cups 31	13. Ham and Cheese Breakfast Rolls 36
5. Breakfast Meatballs..................... 32	14. Carnivore Breakfast Pizza 36
6. Chicken Sausages........................ 32	15. Beef and Cheese Omelette............... 37
7. Scotch Eggs 33	16. Shrimp and Bacon Skewers............. 37
8. Beef Liver and Egg Scramble 33	17. Chicken Heart and Egg Skewers 38
9. Pork Breakfast Tacos 34	18. Turkey Heart and Scallop Scramble.... 38

CHAPTER 9: POULTRY, TURKEY & DUCK 39

19. Seasoned Chicken Drumsticks 40	28. Cutlets Stuffed with Bacon & Cheese ... 44
20. Chicken Thighs 40	29. Chicken Soufflé 45
21. Turkey Breast 41	30. Turkey Muffins 45
22. Chicken Roulade 41	31. Parmesan Baked Duck.........................46
23. Smoked Chicken 42	32. Chicken Cutlets with Cottage Cheese.........46

24. Turkey Bacon Medallions 42
25. Quail with Herb Butter 43
26. Turkey Turrets 43
27. Crispy Duck Breast 44

33. Turkey and Cheese Pie 47
34. Smoked Turkey Legs 47
35. Chicken Legs Wrapped in Bacon 48
36. Creamy Chicken Breast 48

CHAPTER 10: BEEF, LAMB, PORK, ETC 49

37. Pork Chops with Herb Crust 50
38. Rack of Lamb 50
39. Lamb and Feta Patties 51
40. Lamb Kebab 51
41. Glazed Ribs 52
42. Ribeye Steak 52
43. Carnivore Burger 53
44. Ground Pork Frittata 54
45. T-Bone Steak 54
46. Bone-in Pork Cutlets 55
47. Elk Steak 55
48. Filet Mignon 56

49. New York Strip Steak 56
50. Bison Meatloaf 57
51. Bacon-Wrapped Pork Tenderloin 57
52. Braised Rabbit Pie 58
53. Whiskey Marinated Beef 59
54. Escalope of Lamb 60
55. Beef Steaks in Hot Sauce 60
56. Breaded Pork Steak 61
57. Meatloaf 62
58. Beef with Egg Butter Sauce 63
59. Bison Blue Cheese Burgers 64

CHAPTER 11: FISH & SEAFOOD 65

60. Salmon in Sour Cream Sauce 66
61. Fishcakes 66
62. Lobster in Butter Sauce 67
63. Octopus 67
64. Crab Stuffed Squid 68
65. Squid in Sauce 69
66. Cod with Pesto 69
67. Seafood Stew 70
68. Smoked Crab 71
69. Oyster in Spicy Sauce 71
70. Shrimp in Cheese Sauce 72

71. Cheesy Crusted Salmon 73
72. Ebi Tempura Shrimp 73
73. Mixed Seafood Kebabs 74
74. King Prawn Scampi 74
75. Cream Cheese Salmon Tempura 75
76. Panko Crusted Langoustines 76
77. Scallops in Sour Cream Sauce 76
78. Herbed Baked Pollock 77
79. Mussels with Cheese 77
80. Battered Shrimp Cheese Balls 78

CHAPTER 12: ORGAN MEATS 79

81. Beef Heart Skewers 80
82. Chicken Pate 80
83. Braised Turkey Gizzards 81
84. Poached Beef Tongue with Gravy 81
85. Battered Pork Kidneys with Soy Sauce 82

86. Chicken Offal 82
87. Bacon Pate 83
88. Veal Heart Roast 83
89. Chicken Gizzard Roast 84
90. Liver Pancakes 84

CHAPTER 13: SNACKS & APPETIZERS 85

91. Chicken Wings 86
92. Pork Rinds 86
93. Deviled Eggs 87
94. Sausage Bites 87
95. Mozzarella Sticks 88

96. Cheese Crisps 88
97. Flavorful Air Fryer Jerky 89
98. Beef Liver Chips 89
99. Ham Croquettes 90
100. Glazed Shrimp Skewers 90

CHAPTER 14: TOP 10 QUESTIONS AND ANSWERS ABOUT THE CARNIVORE DIET 91
42 DAY MEAL PLAN 93
COOKING CONVERSION CHART 96
CONCLUSION 97

INTRODUCTION

Welcome to "The Carnivore Diet Air Fryer cookbook" a unique cookbook that combines the simplicity and efficiency of the carnivore lifestyle with the modern convenience of an air fryer. Designed for those who crave delicious meat-centric meals, this cookbook offers a variety of recipes to cater to all your carnivore cravings, whether you're a seasoned carnivore or just starting your journey.

The carnivore diet focuses on animal-based foods, emphasizing high-quality proteins and healthy fats. Many people experience improved digestion, mental clarity, and sustained energy by eliminating plant-based foods. This cookbook combines these dietary principles with the innovative air fryer, a kitchen appliance that has revolutionized home cooking by offering a healthier, faster, and cleaner way to prepare meals.

You can achieve perfectly crispy and tender meats using an air fryer without the excess oils or lengthy cooking times traditionally associated with frying. It's a game-changer for anyone looking to streamline their cooking process while enjoying flavorful and satisfying dishes. As you flip through these pages, you'll find inspiration in the variety and versatility of the recipes. Whether you're in the mood for a quick weeknight dinner or planning a feast for special occasions, you'll find the perfect dish to satisfy your appetite. The carnivore diet is often perceived as restrictive, but this cookbook proves it can be diverse, exciting, and incredibly delicious.

In addition to recipes, you'll find helpful tips on sourcing the best quality meats, understanding different cuts, and mastering air fryer techniques. The goal is to make your carnivore diet journey as enjoyable and hassle-free as possible. By the end of this book, you'll be equipped with the knowledge and skills to create meals that are nutritious and a delight to your taste buds.

Prepare to embark on a culinary adventure that will redefine how you think about meat and cooking.

CHAPTER 1:
OVERVIEW AND PRINCIPLES OF THE CARNIVORE DIET

The carnivore diet, often called the carnivore diet, is a nutritional approach that focuses exclusively on animal-based foods. This dietary lifestyle is rooted in the idea that humans thrive on a diet primarily composed of meat and animal products, which provide essential nutrients in their most bioavailable forms. By eliminating plant-based foods, proponents of the carnivore diet aim to optimize health, improve digestion, and reduce inflammation.

Core Principles

Animal-Based Nutrition: The foundation of the carnivore diet is consuming animal products exclusively. This includes all types of meat, fish, eggs, and dairy (if tolerated). The emphasis is on nutrient-dense foods that are rich in protein, healthy fats, vitamins, and minerals. This ensures that you are getting all the necessary nutrients for your body to function at its best.

Elimination of Plant Foods: By removing all plant-based foods, including fruits, vegetables, grains, and legumes, the diet aims to reduce exposure to potential antinutrients and allergens that some individuals may be sensitive to. This can lead to improved digestion and reduced gastrointestinal issues.

High-Quality Protein: Protein is a critical component of the carnivore diet. High-quality protein sources, such as beef, pork, poultry, and fish, provide the essential amino acids necessary for muscle growth, repair, and overall bodily function.

Healthy Fats: The diet encourages the consumption of healthy animal fats, crucial for hormone production, brain health, and energy. These fats include those found in fatty meat, butter, ghee, and lard cuts.

Nutrient Density: Animal foods are incredibly nutrient-dense, offering many vitamins and minerals. For example, organ meats like liver are particularly rich in vitamins A, B, and D and minerals like iron and zinc.

Satiety and Simplicity: The carnivore diet is known for its simplicity and satiating nature. High-protein and high-fat meals help to keep you full and satisfied for longer periods, reducing the need for frequent snacking and potentially aiding in weight management. This simplicity makes it easier to adopt and maintain, allowing you to focus on other aspects of your life without the constant worry of meal planning.

1.1 What are the main benefits of the carnivore diet?

The carnivore diet, which focuses exclusively on animal-based foods, offers a range of benefits that many followers find transformative. This dietary approach can provide several health advantages by eliminating plant-based foods and focusing on nutrient-dense meats. Here are the main benefits of the carnivore diet:

Improved Digestion: One of the carnivore diet's most notable benefits is improved digestion. Many individuals who switch to this diet report relief from common gastrointestinal issues such as bloating, gas, and irritable bowel syndrome (IBS). By eliminating plant-based foods, which can contain antinutrients and fibers that some people find hard to digest, the carnivore diet can help streamline digestive processes and reduce discomfort.

Enhanced Mental Clarity: Another significant advantage is enhanced mental clarity. The carnivore diet can help stabilize blood sugar levels and reduce inflammation, contributing to better cognitive function. Many followers experience improved focus, concentration, and overall mental sharpness.

Sustained Energy Levels: The high-fat content of the carnivore diet provides a steady source of energy throughout the day. Unlike carbohydrates, which can cause energy spikes and crashes, fats offer a more consistent energy supply. This can increase stamina and reduce fatigue, making it easier to maintain an active lifestyle.

Weight Management: Weight management is a common goal, and the carnivore diet can be particularly effective. High-protein and high-fat meals promote satiety, helping to reduce overall calorie intake by keeping you full and satisfied for extended periods. This can naturally lead to weight loss or maintenance without constant snacking or calorie counting.

Reduced Inflammation: Inflammation is at the root of many chronic diseases; the carnivore diet can help reduce it. The diet can lower systemic inflammation levels by cutting out potential inflammatory foods such as grains, legumes, and certain vegetables. This may result in improved symptoms for conditions like arthritis, autoimmune diseases, and skin disorders.

Better Blood Sugar Control: The carnivore diet's emphasis on proteins and fats helps to regulate blood sugar levels more effectively than a carbohydrate-heavy diet. This can be particularly beneficial for individuals with insulin resistance or diabetes, as it reduces the risk of blood sugar spikes and crashes.

Simplicity and Convenience: The carnivore diet is inherently simple, focusing on a narrow range of food options. This simplicity can simplify meal planning and preparation, saving time and effort. Additionally, using an air fryer can further streamline cooking processes, making it easier to stick to the diet.

Reduction in Food Cravings: The carnivore diet can help reduce cravings, particularly for sugary and processed foods, by providing the body with adequate protein and healthy fats. This can lead to more stable eating patterns and better overall dietary adherence.

Hormonal Balance: Animal-based foods are rich in nutrients that support hormonal health. The carnivore diet can help balance hormones, which is crucial for overall well-being. Improved hormone levels can improve mood, energy, and metabolic function.

1.2 Who may need a carnivore diet?

The carnivore diet, focusing exclusively on animal-based foods, is only for some. Still, it can be particularly beneficial for certain individuals facing specific health challenges or looking to achieve particular health goals. Here are some groups who might need or benefit from a carnivore diet:

Those Seeking Weight Loss

The carnivore diet can serve as a powerful tool for individuals struggling with weight loss. Meals rich in protein and fat promote a feeling of fullness, reducing the urge for frequent snacking. This, in turn, aids in calorie control and the achievement of weight loss goals.

Those Looking for Simplified Nutrition

The carnivore diet offers simplicity for individuals who prefer a straightforward approach to eating without the complexity of counting calories or macronutrients. Focusing solely on animal-based foods simplifies meal planning and preparation, making a consistent and healthy diet more manageable.

1.3 Common Misconceptions About the Carnivore Diet

While gaining popularity, the carnivore diet must be more understood and surrounded by various misconceptions. Clarifying these myths can help you make informed decisions and better understand the principles behind this dietary approach. Here are some common misconceptions about the carnivore diet:

Misconception 1: Lack of Essential Nutrients

One prevalent myth is that the carnivore diet lacks essential nutrients, particularly vitamins and minerals, in plant-based foods. However, animal-based foods are nutrient-dense and can provide all necessary nutrients when consumed in a variety. For instance, organ meats like liver are rich in vitamins A, B, D, and K, while muscle meats provide ample protein, iron, and zinc.

Misconception 2: High Cholesterol and Heart Disease

Many people believe that a diet high in animal fats will lead to high cholesterol levels and heart disease. Recent studies have shown that dietary cholesterol has a minimal impact on blood cholesterol levels for most people. Moreover, the carnivore diet often leads to improved markers of heart health, such as reduced triglycerides and increased HDL (good) cholesterol levels.

Misconception 3: Unsustainable Long-Term

Some argue that the carnivore diet is unsustainable in the long term due to its restrictive nature. However, many followers report high levels of satisfaction and adherence to the diet. The key is variety within the allowable foods and finding delicious, creative ways to prepare meals, such as using an air fryer to enhance flavors and textures.

Misconception 4: Limited Food Choices

Another common belief is that the carnivore diet is monotonous and lacks variety. In reality, there is a wide range of animal-based foods to enjoy, including different cuts of beef, pork, poultry, fish, seafood, eggs, and dairy (if tolerated). Additionally, incorporating various cooking methods and seasonings can keep meals exciting and satisfying.

Misconception 5: Only Suitable for Weight Loss

While weight loss is a significant benefit for many on the carnivore diet, it's not the only advantage. This diet can also improve mental clarity, energy levels, and digestive health and reduce inflammation. Many people adopt the carnivore diet for these health benefits beyond weight management.

Misconception 6: Lack of Fiber is Harmful

Concerns about fiber intake are common, as traditional dietary guidelines emphasize its importance. However, many individuals on the carnivore diet experience improved digestive health despite the lack of fiber. This may be due to reducing plant-based fibers and antinutrients that can cause digestive issues for some people.

Misconception 7: Difficulty in Social Situations

It's often thought that the carnivore diet is impractical in social settings. While challenging, planning and choosing suitable options at restaurants or social gatherings can make it manageable. Many restaurants offer meat-focused dishes that can fit within the carnivore diet framework.

CHAPTER 2: BEGINNING A CARNIVORE DIET

Embarking on a carnivore diet is a bold step towards a new eating method focusing exclusively on animal-based foods. This chapter will guide you through the fundamentals of starting a carnivore diet, offering practical tips and insights to ensure a smooth transition. You'll learn how to prepare your kitchen, plan your meals, and utilize your air fryer to its fullest potential. The carnivore diet offers numerous health benefits, including improved energy levels, digestion, and weight management. However, it's essential to approach this diet with knowledge and preparation to reap the maximum benefits while minimizing potential challenges. Let's dive in and explore how you can start your journey on a carnivore diet and make delicious, nutrient-dense meals using your air fryer.

2.1 Three critical steps to switch to a carnivore diet

Switching to a carnivore diet requires careful planning and a gradual adjustment period. Here are three important steps to help you make the transition smoothly:

1. Gradual Elimination
Start by gradually reducing your intake of plant-based foods. This slow transition allows your body to adapt to the increasing proportion of animal-based foods. Begin by cutting out processed foods, grains, and sugars, then slowly eliminate vegetables and fruits. This step-by-step approach can help prevent digestive discomfort and make the switch more manageable.

2. Focus on Nutrient-Dense Meats
Incorporate a variety of nutrient-dense meats into your diet. Aim for a balance of lean and fatty cuts, and include organ meats like liver and heart, which are rich in essential vitamins and minerals. Prioritize high-quality, grass-fed, pasture-raised meats whenever possible to ensure you get the best nutrition.

3. Optimize Cooking Techniques
Use your air fryer effectively to prepare delicious and healthy carnivore meals. The air fryer can be a versatile tool for cooking meat, offering a convenient way to achieve crispy, flavorful results without excess oil. Experiment with different recipes and techniques to find the best for your taste and dietary needs.

2.2. Understand the physical and psychological changes you may experience during transition

Understand the physical and psychological changes you may experience during transition
Transitioning to a carnivore diet can bring about several physical and psychological changes. It's essential to be aware of these potential shifts to manage them effectively:

1. Physical Changes

Digestive Adjustments: As your body adapts to a meat-only diet, you might experience changes in digestion. Some people report initial digestive discomfort, such as constipation or diarrhea, which usually resolves as your body adjusts.

Energy Levels: You may notice fluctuations in your energy levels during the transition's initial stages. Some individuals experience an initial dip in energy as their bodies switch from burning carbohydrates to fats for fuel, followed by a boost in sustained energy.

Weight Changes: Weight loss is a common outcome for many people on a carnivore diet, mainly if they previously consumed high amounts of carbohydrates. This can be due to both fat loss and reduced water weight.

2. Psychological Changes

Embracing mental Clarity: A significant number of individuals report enhanced mental clarity and focus after transitioning to a carnivore diet. This could be attributed to the stabilization of blood sugar levels and the elimination of processed foods and sugars. Highlighting these potential benefits can motivate you to continue the transition despite potential mood swings.

Mood Swings: Some individuals might experience mood swings during the transition period. This can be attributed to the body's adjustment to a new fuel source and the detoxification from sugar and processed food addiction.

Cravings and Addictions: The patient is expected to experience cravings for carbohydrates and sugary foods, especially in the beginning. Understanding that these cravings are part of the adaptation process can help you stay committed to your new diet.

Empowering Yourself: being prepared for these physical and psychological changes is essential. It can help you navigate the transition more smoothly and stay committed to your carnivore diet. Remember, each person's experience is unique, and it's crucial to listen to your body and adjust as needed. This empowerment allows you to take control of your transition process.

2.3 Effective tips will help maintain nutritional balance and long-term adherence to the diet

Maintaining nutritional balance and long-term adherence to a carnivore diet requires mindful planning and consistency. Here are some practical tips to help you stay on track:

1. Variety is Key
Ensure you consume a variety of meats to get a broad spectrum of nutrients. Include different cuts of beef, pork, lamb, poultry, and seafood. Remember organ meats, which are rich in vitamins and minerals.

2. Prioritize Quality
Choose high-quality, grass-fed, and pasture-raised meats whenever possible. These options are often more nutrient-dense and free from hormones and antibiotics that can be found in conventionally raised meats.

3. Balance Your Fats
Include both fatty and lean cuts of meat in your diet. Fat is an essential energy source on a carnivore diet, but balance is important to avoid digestive issues and ensure adequate protein intake.

4. Stay Hydrated
Drinking water is crucial, as a meat-based diet can be a diuretic. Proper hydration supports kidney function and overall health. Consider adding electrolytes if you experience symptoms of dehydration, such as headaches or fatigue.

5. Listen to Your Body
Pay attention to how your body responds to different meat and meal frequencies. Adjust your diet based on energy levels, digestion, and overall well-being. Your body's needs may change, so stay flexible and responsive.

6. Plan and Prep Meals
Meal planning and preparation can help you stay consistent with your diet. Use your air fryer to make quick, delicious, and healthy meals. Batch cooking and storing meals can save time and prevent the temptation to stray from your diet.

7. Monitor Your Health
Regular check-ins with a healthcare provider help ensure you're maintaining a healthy nutritional balance. Blood tests can monitor cholesterol levels, kidney function, and other important health markers.

8. Join a Community
Connecting with others who follow a carnivore diet can provide support, share recipes, and offer encouragement. Online forums and local groups can be great resources for advice and motivation.

2.4 Safety considerations and health effects

Embarking on a carnivore diet involves understanding the safety considerations and potential health effects. Here are some key points to keep in mind:

1. Consult with a Healthcare Provider
Before starting a carnivore diet, consult with a healthcare provider to ensure it suits you, especially if you have pre-existing health conditions or are taking medications. Remember, your healthcare provider is there to support you and address any concerns that may arise.

2. Monitor Cholesterol and Heart Health
A diet high in animal fats can affect cholesterol levels. Regular blood tests to monitor cholesterol and other lipid levels can help ensure you maintain heart health. Remember, you are in control of your health journey. Some individuals may experience improved cholesterol profiles, while others might see an increase, so individual monitoring is crucial.

3. Kidney Function
High protein intake can impact kidney function, especially in individuals with pre-existing kidney conditions. Ensure adequate hydration and consider regular kidney function tests to monitor any changes.

4. Electrolyte Balance
Meat-based diets can lead to electrolyte imbalances, particularly in the initial stages. Symptoms such as headaches, muscle cramps, and fatigue can indicate electrolyte deficiencies. Adding salt to your meals and considering electrolyte supplements can help maintain balance.

5. Digestive Health
Transitioning to a carnivore diet can cause digestive changes, such as constipation or diarrhea. Staying hydrated, including fatty and lean meats, and gradually adjusting to the diet can help manage these issues. Some people find that including bone broth or organ meats improves digestive health.

6. Nutrient Deficiencies
While meat is nutrient-dense, specific vitamins and minerals like Vitamin C and fiber are absent. Consider supplements or carefully planned inclusion of organ meats to prevent deficiencies. Regular nutritional assessments can help identify and address any gaps.

7. Long-term Health Effects
The long-term health effects of a carnivore diet are still being studied. Anecdotal evidence suggests benefits such as weight loss, improved mental clarity, and reduced inflammation. However, staying informed about new research and adapting your diet as needed is essential.

Understanding these safety considerations and potential health effects can help you make informed decisions and maintain a balanced, healthy approach to the carnivore diet. Regular monitoring and consultation with healthcare professionals are vital to ensuring this diet benefits you.

CHAPTER 3:
PERMITTED AND PROHIBITED PRODUCTS

Understanding which foods are allowed and which are prohibited is essential for following a carnivore diet. This section will guide you through the foods you can enjoy and those you should avoid. By focusing on high-quality animal-based foods, you can ensure you're getting the necessary nutrients while staying true to the principles of the carnivore diet.

3.1 Allowed products

When following the carnivore diet, focusing on high-quality animal-based foods is essential. This diet allows meats, including beef, pork, poultry, and seafood. Beef is a cornerstone, with ribeye, sirloin, and brisket offering rich flavors and nutrients. Ground beef is also versatile for making burgers and meatballs. Pork options, such as pork chops, bacon, and pork shoulder, are delicious and satisfying, while pork belly can be deep-fried for a crispy treat.

Poultry, including chicken thighs, drumsticks, breasts, and turkey and duck, provide a range of textures and tastes. Seafood lovers can enjoy fish like salmon, mackerel, and sardines and shellfish like shrimp, crab, and lobster. Oysters are a nutrient-dense choice, rich in zinc.

Organ meats, a highly recommended part of the carnivore diet, are a nutritional powerhouse. Incorporating liver, kidneys, and heart into your diet provides an extra boost of vitamins and minerals, ensuring you're getting the most out of your meals. Remember to mention bone marrow, which has a rich flavor and health benefits. It's another excellent option to consider.

If you tolerate dairy, include hard cheeses, grass-fed butter, and heavy cream. Eggs are also a staple, offering versatility and nutrition, with free-range or pasture-raised being the best choice.

By focusing on these allowed products, you're not just following a diet, you're creating a diverse and nutrient-rich menu that aligns with the carnivore diet. And with the freedom to explore different cooking methods, like making the most of your deep fryer, you're empowered to make your carnivore journey a creative and exciting one.

3.2 Foods that should be excluded from the diet

Embracing a carnivore diet involves the exclusion of all plant-based foods. This means bidding farewell to fruits and vegetables, even the seemingly healthy ones like leafy greens, berries, and cruciferous vegetables. Grains, including wheat, rice, oats, and corn, are also a no-go, as their high carbohydrate content can disrupt the metabolic state encouraged by a carnivore diet. However, this dietary shift can lead to significant health benefits, such as improved metabolic health and weight management.

Legumes, such as beans, lentils, and chickpeas, are excluded due to their carbohydrate content and potential to cause digestive issues for some individuals. All forms of sugar and sweeteners, both natural and artificial, should be avoided to maintain stable blood sugar levels and promote metabolic health.

Processed foods are strictly prohibited. This includes snacks, baked goods, and convenience foods, often containing hidden sugars, unhealthy fats, and additives incompatible with a predatory lifestyle. Vegetable oils, such as canola, soybean, and corn oil, should be replaced with animal fats like lard, tallow, and duck fat, which are more suitable for deep frying and align with the diet's principles.

While sometimes included in moderation, dairy products should be limited to those who can tolerate them without digestive distress. Items like milk, yogurt, and soft cheeses may be excluded to avoid potential issues with lactose and casein.

Alcohol is a category that should be avoided in a carnivore diet. It can interfere with metabolic processes and add unnecessary carbohydrates to your diet. However, it's essential to note that not all beverages are off-limits. For instance, soda, juice, and energy drinks, which contain high levels of sugar and artificial ingredients, should be eliminated. But, if you choose to consume alcohol, it's best to opt for low-carb options and drink in moderation.

Lastly, it's essential to avoid plant-derived condiments and sauces, which often contain sugars, oils, and other additives that do not fit into the carnivore framework. Instead, focus on seasoning your meats with simple, natural spices and herbs that do not contain added fillers or preservatives.

By excluding these foods from your diet, you can better adhere to the carnivore lifestyle and fully embrace its health benefits, particularly when preparing your meals with a deep fryer.

CHAPTER 4: USING AN AIR FRYER ON A CARNIVORE DIET

Incorporating an air fryer into your carnivore diet can enhance your culinary experience by providing a convenient and healthy way to prepare your favorite meat-based dishes. Here are some tips and techniques for making the most of your air fryer:

1. Choosing the Right Cuts of Meat
Opt for cuts that will cook evenly and retain moisture. Thick cuts like ribeye steaks, pork chops, and chicken thighs are ideal for air frying. These cuts will stay juicy on the inside while developing a crispy exterior.

2. Preheating the Air Fryer
Always preheat your air fryer before adding the meat. This ensures the cooking surface is hot enough to sear the meat, locking in juices and flavor. A preheated air fryer also helps achieve a more even cook.

3. Seasoning and Marinating
Keep seasonings simple to highlight the natural flavors of the meat. Salt, pepper, garlic powder, and herbs are great options. For added flavor, marinate your meat for a few hours or overnight using simple, carnivore-friendly ingredients like lemon juice, vinegar, and olive oil.

4. Using the Right Temperature and Timing
Each type of meat requires different temperature settings and cooking times. For example, beef steaks are best cooked at high temperatures (around 400°F) for shorter periods (10-15 minutes), while chicken may need lower temperatures (375°F) for longer times (20-25 minutes). Refer to your air fryer's manual for specific guidelines.

5. Avoiding Overcrowding
Do not overcrowd the air fryer basket. Ensure enough space between each piece of meat for air to circulate correctly. Overcrowding can lead to uneven cooking and less crispy results.

6. Checking for Doneness
Use a meat thermometer to check the internal temperature of your meat. This ensures it is cooked to your preferred level of doneness. For example, beef steaks are typically medium-rare at 135°F, while chicken should reach 165°F for safe consumption.

7. Resting the Meat
Allow your meat to rest for a few minutes after air frying. This helps redistribute the juices, resulting in a more flavorful and tender bite. Cover the meat loosely with foil to keep it warm

8. Experimenting with Recipes

Don't be afraid to experiment with different cuts and recipes. The air fryer is versatile and can handle a variety of meats, from juicy burgers to crispy pork belly. Explore marinades, seasonings, and cooking techniques to find what you enjoy most.

By mastering these techniques, you can enjoy delicious, perfectly cooked meat dishes while adhering to your carnivore diet. The air fryer makes it easy to prepare healthy and satisfying meals, ensuring you stay on track with your dietary goals.

4.1 Benefits of using an air fryer in a Carnivore diet

Using an air fryer as part of your carnivore diet offers several advantages, enhancing both the quality of your meals and the convenience of your cooking process. Here are the key benefits:

1. Healthier Cooking Method

The air fryer uses hot air circulation to cook food to achieve a crispy exterior without excessive oil. This method reduces the intake of added fats and calories, making it a healthier option than traditional deep frying.

2. Retains Nutrients

Air frying preserves the nutrients in your meat by cooking it quickly and efficiently. The high heat and rapid cooking time helps lock in essential vitamins and minerals, ensuring you get the most nutritional benefit from your meals.

3. Crispy Texture Without the Guilt

One of the highlights of using an air fryer is enjoying a crispy texture without the guilt associated with deep frying. You can savor deliciously crispy bacon, chicken wings, and pork rinds without compromising your health goals.

4. Convenience and Speed

Air fryers are incredibly convenient, offering a quick and easy way to prepare your meals. They preheat faster and cook more rapidly than traditional ovens, making it easier to whip up a nutritious carnivore meal in less time.

5. Versatility in Cooking

The air fryer is versatile and can handle a wide range of meats. You can experiment with different cuts and recipes, from steaks and chops to burgers and fish. It's also great for reheating leftovers and maintaining their taste and texture.

6. Less Mess and Cleanup

Cooking with an air fryer typically involves less mess compared to deep frying. The enclosed cooking space reduces splatters, and many air fryer components are dishwasher safe, simplifying the cleanup process.

7. Energy Efficiency

Air fryers are more energy-efficient than conventional ovens. They use less electricity and produce less heat, which can be beneficial during hot weather, helping to keep your kitchen cooler.

8. Enhanced Flavor

The rapid air circulation in an air fryer can enhance the flavor of your meat by creating a perfectly seared crust while keeping the inside juicy and tender. This cooking method can bring out the best in high-quality cuts of meat.

9. Portion Control

Using an air fryer can help with portion control, as the cooking basket size naturally limits the amount of food you prepare at one time. This can be useful for managing your intake and ensuring balanced meals.

10. Experimentation and Creativity

An air fryer encourages culinary creativity, allowing you to experiment with various marinades, seasonings, and cooking techniques. This can make your carnivore diet more enjoyable and sustainable in the long term.

By incorporating an air fryer into your carnivore diet, you can enjoy these benefits and make your cooking experience healthier and more enjoyable.

4.2 Air fryer maintenance and safety tips

Proper maintenance and adherence to safety guidelines are crucial for getting the most out of your air fryer and ensuring its longevity. Here are some essential tips to help you maintain and safely use your air fryer while following a carnivore diet:

1. Regular Cleaning

After each use, clean the air fryer basket, tray, and pan. Most components are dishwasher safe, but always check the manufacturer's instructions. Use warm, soapy water and a non-abrasive sponge for hand washing to avoid damaging the non-stick coating.

2. Avoid Overcrowding

Do not overcrowd the air fryer basket. Overcrowding can lead to uneven cooking and reduce the efficiency of the air fryer. Cook in batches if necessary to ensure even air circulation and crispy results.

3. Use Appropriate Utensils

Use silicone, wooden, or plastic utensils to avoid scratching the non-stick surface of your air fryer. Metal utensils can damage the coating and reduce the appliance's lifespan.

4. Check and Replace Parts as Needed
Regularly inspect the air fryer's components, such as the basket and tray, for signs of wear and tear. Replace any damaged parts to ensure the appliance functions safely and efficiently.

5. Preheat When Required
Preheat your air fryer when the recipe calls for it. Preheating ensures the appliance reaches the optimal temperature for cooking, leading to better results and reduced cooking time.

6. Monitor Cooking Progress
Keep an eye on your food as it cooks. While air fryers are designed to be relatively safe, it's still essential to monitor cooking progress to prevent overcooking or burning.

7. Safe Placement and Ventilation
Place your air fryer on a flat, heat-resistant surface. Ensure there is adequate ventilation around the appliance to prevent overheating. Do not place it near flammable materials or under overhead cabinets while in use.

8. Use Proper Settings
Follow the recommended temperature and time settings for different types of meat. Each cut of meat may require different settings to achieve optimal results, so refer to your air fryer's manual and recipe guidelines.

9. Avoid Using Aerosol Cooking Sprays
Aerosol cooking sprays can damage the non-stick coating of the air fryer basket. Instead, use a brush or a pump spray bottle to apply oil.

10. Unplug When Not in Use
Always unplug the air fryer when it is not in use. This helps prevent electrical hazards and conserves energy.

11. Handle with Care
When removing the basket or tray, use oven mitts or heat-resistant gloves to protect your hands from burns. The interior components can become very hot during cooking.

12. Follow the Manufacturer's Instructions
Always follow the manufacturer's instructions and guidelines for operating and maintaining your air fryer. This ensures safe use and optimal performance of the appliance.

4.3 Temperature and Time Guide for Air Frying Meat

One key aspect of mastering the art of air-frying meat is temperature control. It's crucial to understand the right temperatures and cooking times to achieve perfect results. For instance, beef, such as ribeye and sirloin, should be cooked at 400°F for about 10-15 minutes, depending on the desired doneness. Similarly, ground beef patties can be air-fried at the same temperature for 8-12 minutes.

Chicken requires a slightly lower temperature; cook thighs, drumsticks, and breasts at 375°F for 20-25 minutes. For crispy chicken wings, 400°F for 20 minutes works well. Pork chops are best air-fried at 400°F for 12-15 minutes, while pork tenderloin benefits from 375°F for 25-30 minutes.

When air frying fish fillets like salmon and trout, it's recommended to set the temperature at 375°F for 10-12 minutes. This ensures they remain tender and flaky. For shellfish like shrimp, a temperature of 400°F for 8-10 minutes is ideal. Remember, always use a meat thermometer to check for the appropriate internal temperature: 145°F for beef, pork, and fish; 165°F for poultry. This not only guarantees food safety but also ensures the meat is cooked to the optimal taste.

By following these guidelines, you can use your air fryer to achieve perfectly cooked meat every time, enhancing your carnivore diet with delicious, nutritious meals.

CHAPTER 5:
TYPES OF STEAKS AND THEIR PREPARATION

Different types of steaks offer unique flavors and textures, making them a versatile choice for your carnivore diet. Here are some popular types of steaks, all prepared from beef, and tips for cooking them in an air fryer with accurate cooking times:

5.1 An overview of the different types of steak, with tips for selecting and preparing each cut for optimal flavor and nutritional value

1. Ribeye
Description: Ribeye is a tender and flavorful cut known for its rich marbling.
Cooking: Preheat your air fryer to 400°F. Season the steak with salt and pepper or your favorite steak seasoning. Cook for 12-15 minutes, flipping halfway through, until the internal temperature reaches 135°F for medium-rare. Let it rest for a few minutes before serving.

2. Sirloin
Description: A leaner cut with a firm texture, sirloin is both flavorful and versatile.
Cooking: Preheat your air fryer to 400°F—season with salt, pepper, and garlic powder. Cook for 10-12 minutes, flipping halfway through, until the internal temperature reaches 135°F for medium-rare. Allow the steak to rest before serving.

3. Filet Mignon
Description: The most tender cut, filet mignon, is lean and mild in flavor.
Cooking: Preheat your air fryer to 400°F—season with salt and pepper. Cook for 10-12 minutes, flipping halfway through, until the internal temperature reaches 135°F for medium-rare. Let it rest for a few minutes before serving.

4. New York Strip
Description: Known for its balance of tenderness and flavor, with a fine grain and good marbling.
Cooking: Preheat your air fryer to 400°F—season with salt, pepper, and olive oil. Cook for 12-15 minutes, flipping halfway through, until the internal temperature reaches 135°F for medium-rare. Allow the steak to rest before serving.

5. T-Bone
Description: Combines the flavors of the strip and tenderloin, offering the best of both worlds.

Cooking: Preheat your air fryer to 400°F—season with salt and pepper. Cook for 15-18 minutes, flipping halfway through, until the internal temperature reaches 135°F for medium-rare. Let it rest for a few minutes before serving.

6. Flank Steak

Description: A lean, flavorful cut often used for fajitas and stir-fries.
Cooking: Preheat your air fryer to 400°F. Marinate in olive oil, soy sauce, and garlic for added flavor. Cook for 8-10 minutes, flipping halfway through, until the internal temperature reaches 135°F for medium-rare. Slice thinly against the grain before serving.

7. Porterhouse

Description: Similar to the T-bone but with a more significant portion of tenderloin, offering a substantial and satisfying meal.
Cooking: Preheat your air fryer to 400°F—season generously with salt and pepper. Cook for 15-20 minutes, flipping halfway through, until the internal temperature reaches 135°F for medium-rare. Allow the steak to rest before serving.

By following these cooking tips, you can enjoy a variety of perfectly cooked beef steaks using your air fryer, enhancing the flavors and textures to suit your carnivore diet.

5.2 The importance of grass-fed meat

Choosing grass-fed meat can significantly enhance your carnivore diet's health benefits and flavor. Here's why opting for grass-fed over conventionally raised meat is essential:

1. Nutritional Superiority

Grass-fed meat is richer in essential nutrients compared to grain-fed beef. It contains higher levels of omega-3 fatty acids, which are crucial for heart health and reducing inflammation. Additionally, grass-fed beef boasts higher concentrations of vitamins A and E, antioxidants, and minerals like zinc, iron, and selenium.

2. Better Fat Profile

The fat composition of grass-fed meat is more favorable. It has a higher ratio of healthy fats, including conjugated linoleic acid (CLA), linked to various health benefits like improved immune function and reduced body fat. The lower levels of unhealthy saturated fats also contribute to better overall health.

3. Free from Hormones and Antibiotics

Grass-fed animals are typically raised without growth hormones and antibiotics, which are commonly used in conventional farming to promote rapid growth and prevent disease. This means grass-fed meat is free from these potentially harmful additives, resulting in a cleaner, more natural product.

4. Enhanced Flavor and Texture

Many people find that grass-fed meat has a superior flavor and texture compared to grain-fed beef. The natural diet of grasses and forage that grass-fed animals consume contributes to a richer, more complex taste and a firmer texture, enhancing the culinary experience of your carnivore meals.

5. Environmental Benefits

Grass-fed farming practices are generally more sustainable and environmentally friendly. Raising animals on pasture helps maintain healthy soil, promotes biodiversity, and reduces the carbon footprint associated with grain-fed meat production. Supporting grass-fed meat also encourages more ethical and sustainable farming practices.

6. Animal Welfare

Grass-fed animals typically have better living conditions, with more space to roam and engage in natural behaviors. This leads to less stress and a higher quality of life for the animals, aligning with more humane and ethical farming practices.

7. Consistency with Ancestral Diets

Grass-fed meat is closer to what our ancestors consumed, making it a more natural fit for a diet based on evolutionary principles. Eating grass-fed beef aligns with the philosophy of consuming whole, unprocessed foods that our bodies are better adapted to digest and utilize. Incorporating grass-fed meat into your carnivore diet can enhance your meals' nutritional value, flavor, and ethical aspects. Choosing high-quality, grass-fed beef supports your health, the environment, and animal welfare, making it a worthwhile investment for your carnivore lifestyle.

5.3 Benefits of wild fish

Including wild fish in your carnivore diet can offer numerous health benefits, enhancing your meals' nutritional profile and flavor. Here's why wild fish is an excellent choice:

1. Higher Nutrient Density

Wild fish generally have a superior nutrient profile compared to farmed fish. They are richer in essential vitamins and minerals such as vitamin D, B12, iodine, and selenium, which are vital for maintaining overall health and proper bodily functions.

2. Optimal Omega-3 Fatty Acids

Wild fish are an excellent source of omega-3 fatty acids, particularly EPA and DHA, which are crucial for brain health, reducing inflammation, and supporting cardiovascular health. The omega-3 content in wild fish is typically higher and more balanced than in farmed fish.

3. Lower Levels of Contaminants

Wild fish are less likely to contain harmful contaminants such as antibiotics, pesticides, and artificial additives often used in farming. This makes wild fish a cleaner and safer option for consumption.

4. Better Flavor and Texture

Many people find that wild fish have a more robust flavor and firmer texture compared to farmed fish. The natural diet and environment of wild fish contribute to their distinct and superior taste, making carnivore meals more enjoyable.

5. Environmental Sustainability

Wild fish are typically caught using more sustainable practices than fish farming methods, which can be associated with environmental issues like water pollution and habitat destruction. Supporting wild-caught fish helps promote sustainable fishing practices and ocean health.

6. Natural Diet and Behavior

Wild fish consume a natural diet and live in their natural habitats, improving overall health and nutrition. This natural lifestyle results in leaner fish and is free from artificial growth enhancers commonly used in farming.

7. Rich in Antioxidants

Wild fish often have higher levels of antioxidants, such as astaxanthin, particularly in species like salmon. These antioxidants help protect your cells from damage, support skin health, and enhance immune function.

8. Supports Local Economies

Choosing wild-caught fish can support local fishermen and sustainable fishing industries. This contributes to local economies and encourages responsible fishing practices that protect marine ecosystems.

Incorporating wild fish into your carnivore diet provides health benefits, superior flavor, and support for sustainable practices. By opting for wild-caught varieties, you ensure that your meals are nutritious, delicious, and environmentally friendly, making wild fish an excellent addition to your air fryer recipes.

CHAPTER 6:
WHAT IMPORTANT VITAMINS ARE PRESENT IN MEAT

Meat is a powerhouse of essential vitamins crucial in maintaining overall health and well-being. Here are some of the most critical vitamins present in meat and their benefits:

1. Vitamin B12
Importance: Vitamin B12 is vital for red blood cell formation, neurological function, and DNA synthesis. It helps prevent anemia and supports cognitive health.
Sources: Beef, lamb, pork, poultry, and fish.

2. Vitamin B6
Importance: Vitamin B6 supports brain development and function, helps convert food into energy, and produces neurotransmitters and red blood cells.
Sources: Chicken, turkey, beef, pork, and fish.

3. Niacin (Vitamin B3)
Importance: Niacin helps convert food into energy, supports digestive health, and contributes to healthy skin and nerves. It also plays a role in lowering cholesterol levels.
Sources: Beef, pork, chicken, and fish.

4. Riboflavin (Vitamin B2)
Importance: Riboflavin is essential for energy production, cellular function, and the metabolism of fats, drugs, and steroids. It also helps maintain healthy skin and eyes.
Sources: Beef, lamb, pork, and poultry.

5. Thiamine (Vitamin B1)
Importance: Thiamine is crucial for energy metabolism and properly functioning the nervous system, muscles, and heart.
Sources: Pork, beef, and lamb.

6. Vitamin A
Importance: Vitamin A is essential for vision, immune function, and skin health. It also plays a role in reproductive health and cellular communication.
Sources: Liver from beef, lamb, pork, and poultry.

7. Vitamin D
Importance: Vitamin D is essential for calcium absorption and bone health. It also supports immune function and helps regulate mood.
Sources: Fatty fish (such as salmon, mackerel, and sardines), liver, and egg yolks.

8. Vitamin K2
Importance: Vitamin K2 is essential for bone health and helps direct calcium to the bones and teeth instead of soft tissues. It also supports cardiovascular health.
Sources: Liver, beef, pork, chicken, and cheese.

9. Pantothenic Acid (Vitamin B5)
Importance: Pantothenic acid is essential for synthesizing coenzyme A, vital for fatty acid metabolism and energy production.
Sources: Beef, chicken, pork, and fish.

10. Folate (Vitamin B9)
Importance: Folate is crucial for DNA synthesis, repair, and methylation. It also plays a role in cell division and red and white blood cell formation.
Sources: Liver from beef, chicken, and lamb.

These vitamins are integral to numerous bodily functions, from energy production and brain health to immune support and bone strength. Including various meats in your carnivore diet ensures you receive these vital nutrients, contributing to overall health and well-being.

CHAPTER 7:
PROBLEMS THAT MAY ARISE AND THEIR SOLUTIONS

Transitioning to a carnivore diet can bring about various challenges, but these issues can be effectively managed with the right strategies. Here are some common problems and their solutions:

1. Digestive Issues
Problem: Some people experience constipation or diarrhea when switching to a meat-only diet.
Solution: Ensure adequate hydration and consider including bone broth to support gut health. Gradually transition to the diet to allow your digestive system to adapt. Including organ meats can also provide essential nutrients that aid digestion.

2. Electrolyte Imbalance
Problem: The loss of electrolytes, particularly in the initial stages, can cause symptoms like headaches, fatigue, and muscle cramps.
Solution: Increase your electrolyte intake by adding salt to your meals and drinking bone broth. If necessary, consider electrolyte supplements, especially sodium, potassium, and magnesium.

3. Keto Flu
Problem: Symptoms such as fatigue, irritability, and brain fog may occur as your body adapts to burning fat for fuel instead of carbohydrates.
Solution: Stay hydrated, ensure adequate electrolyte intake, and be patient as your body adjusts. Gradually reducing carbohydrates before fully committing to the diet can also help minimize these symptoms.

4. Nutrient Deficiencies
Problem: A restrictive diet can lead to specific vitamin and mineral deficiencies.
Solution: Focus on eating a variety of meats, including nutrient-dense organ meats. Consider supplements for nutrients such as vitamin C that are difficult to obtain from meat alone.

5. Social Challenges
Problem: Eating out or attending social gatherings on a carnivore diet can take time and effort.
Solution: Plan by eating before events or bringing your food. Communicate your dietary needs to friends and family, and look for carnivore-friendly options at restaurants, such as grilled meats.

6. Food Boredom
Problem: Repeatedly eating the same types of meat can lead to boredom and a lack of dietary variety.
Solution: Experiment with different cuts of meat, cooking methods, and seasonings. Use your air fryer to create diverse and delicious meals, such as crispy pork belly, juicy steaks, and flavorful chicken wings.

7. Weight Plateaus
Problem: Weight loss may stall after initial success on the carnivore diet.
Solution: Evaluate your portion sizes and ensure you are not overeating. Incorporate intermittent fasting or adjust your macronutrient ratios by increasing protein intake and reducing fat if needed.

8. Cost Concerns
Problem: High-quality meat can be expensive, making the diet potentially costly.
Solution: Buy in bulk, look for sales, and consider cheaper cuts of meat like ground beef, organ meats, and roasts. Using your air fryer to cook these cuts can make them more enjoyable and tender.

9. Initial Fatigue
Problem: Feeling tired or low in energy during the initial phase of the diet.
Solution: Allow your body time to adapt and ensure you are consuming enough calories and fat for energy. Gradually increasing your activity levels can also help your body adjust.

10. Adaptation Period
Problem: The body may take time to fully adapt to the new diet, leading to temporary discomfort.
Solution: Be patient and give yourself time to adjust. Keep track of your progress and any changes in how you feel. Consulting with a healthcare provider can also provide additional support and guidance during this transition.

By understanding and addressing these potential problems, you can navigate the challenges of a carnivore diet more effectively and enjoy the benefits of this eating approach.

7.1 How to deal with carbohydrate and sugar cravings: effective strategies

Cravings for carbohydrates and sugar can be a significant challenge when transitioning to a carnivore diet. Here are some effective strategies to manage and overcome these cravings:

1. Stay Hydrated
Strategy: Drink plenty of water throughout the day. Sometimes, cravings can be a sign of dehydration. Drinking water can help suppress hunger and reduce the urge for sugary or carb-heavy foods.

2. Eat Sufficient Protein and Fat
Strategy: Ensure you are consuming enough protein and healthy fats. These macronutrients help keep you full and satisfied, reducing cravings. Include fatty cuts of meat, such as ribeye or pork belly, and don't avoid adding healthy animal fats like tallow or butter to your meals.

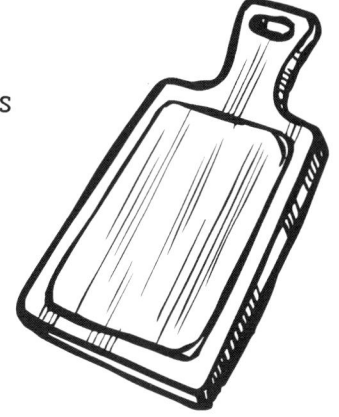

3. Incorporate Nutrient-Dense Foods
Strategy: Include organ meats, such as liver, in your diet. These foods are rich in essential vitamins and minerals, which can help curb cravings by providing your body with the nutrients it needs.

4. Keep Meals Varied and Flavorful
Strategy: Use different cuts of meat and cooking methods to keep your meals interesting. Season your food with herbs and spices that are carnivore-friendly, such as salt, pepper, garlic powder, and paprika, to enhance flavors and reduce the monotony.

5. Address Emotional Triggers
Strategy: Identify emotional triggers that lead to cravings and find alternative ways to cope. Engage in activities you enjoy, such as reading, exercising, or spending time with friends, to distract yourself from cravings.

6. Plan Ahead
Strategy: Prepare carnivore-friendly snacks and meals in advance. Having ready-to-eat options, like beef jerky, hard-boiled eggs, or air-fried meat bites, can help you resist the temptation to reach for carbs or sweets.

7. Gradual Reduction
Strategy: If cravings are intense, consider gradually reducing carbohydrates and sugars rather than eliminating them all at once. This can help your body adjust more comfortably to the new diet.

8. Stay Busy and Active
Strategy: Keep yourself busy with activities and exercise. Physical activity can reduce cravings and help you focus on your dietary goals. Even a short walk can help alleviate the urge to snack.

9. Get Adequate Sleep

Strategy: Ensure you are getting enough sleep each night. Lack of sleep can increase cravings for sugary and high-carb foods. Aim for 7-9 hours of quality sleep per night.

10. Support System

Strategy: Connect with others who are also following a carnivore diet. Join online communities or local support groups where you can share experiences, get advice, and receive encouragement to stay on track.

Implementing these strategies can help you effectively manage carbohydrate and sugar cravings, making it easier to adhere to your carnivore diet and achieve your health goals. experiences, seek advice, and stay motivated. A network of like-minded individuals can make the journey more accessible and enjoyable.

7.2 Identifying and preventing nutritional deficiencies

Ensuring you receive all necessary nutrients is crucial when following a carnivore diet. Focusing on various nutrient-dense foods is essential to recognize and prevent nutrient deficiencies. Include different cuts of meat, such as beef, pork, lamb, and poultry, to cover a broad spectrum of nutrients. Organ meats, like liver and kidneys, are especially rich in vitamins and minerals and should be incorporated regularly.

Monitor for signs of deficiencies, such as fatigue, muscle cramps, and skin issues, which may indicate a lack of essential nutrients. Vitamin D, magnesium, and potassium deficiencies are common concerns. To address these, consider supplements or include foods like fatty fish for vitamin D and organ meats for various minerals. Regularly consult a healthcare provider, consider periodic blood tests to ensure optimal nutrient levels, and adjust your diet.

7.3 Long-term strategies for diet maintenance and transition

Maintaining a carnivore diet over the long term requires careful planning and strategies to ensure sustainability and health. Here are some tips to help you stay on track and make any necessary transitions smoothly:

1. Variety and Creativity
Incorporate various meats to prevent monotony and ensure a broad spectrum of nutrients. Use different cooking methods, including your air fryer, to create diverse and delicious meals. Experiment with various cuts, seasonings, and recipes to keep your diet interesting.

2. Nutrient-Dense Foods
Focus on nutrient-dense foods rich in essential vitamins and minerals, especially organ meats like liver, heart, and kidneys. Including fatty fish such as salmon and mackerel can provide essential omega-3 fatty acids and vitamin D.

3. Regular Monitoring
Regularly monitor your health markers through blood tests to check for nutrient deficiencies or imbalances. Consult a healthcare provider to interpret the results and make necessary dietary adjustments.

4. Adapting to Changes
Be flexible and willing to adapt your diet based on your body's responses and health needs. If you experience any adverse effects, consider incorporating small amounts of non-carnivore foods, such as low-carb vegetables, to see if they help alleviate symptoms.

5. Mindful Eating
Practice mindful eating by listening to your body's hunger and fullness cues. Eating only when hungry and stopping when satisfied can help prevent overeating and promote a healthy relationship with food.

6. Support Systems
Engage with a support system, whether friends, family, or online communities, to share experiences, seek advice, and stay motivated. A network of like-minded individuals can make the journey more accessible and enjoyable.

7. Gradual Transition
If transitioning from or to a different diet, gradually allow your body to adjust. Reintroducing or eliminating foods can help prevent digestive discomfort and smooth the process.

8. Focus on Quality
Prioritize high-quality, grass-fed, and pasture-raised meats whenever possible. These options are often more nutrient-dense and free from harmful additives, supporting overall health and well-being.

CHAPTER 8

BREAKFAST
RECIPES

1. Bacon and Eggs 30
2. Pork Sausage 30
3. Beef Steak and Eggs 31
4. Ham and Egg Cups 31
5. Breakfast Meatballs 32
6. Chicken Sausages 32
7. Scotch Eggs 33
8. Beef Liver and Egg Scramble 33
9. Pork Breakfast Tacos 34

10. Shrimp and Egg Scramble 34
11. Cod and Egg Breakfast Bowls 35
12. Bacon and Steak Frittata 35
13. Ham and Cheese Breakfast Rolls 36
14. Carnivore Breakfast Pizza 36
15. Beef and Cheese Omelette 37
16. Shrimp and Bacon Skewers 37
17. Chicken Heart and Egg Skewers 38
18. Turkey Heart and Scallop Scramble 38

1. Bacon and Eggs

Servings: 4 **Preparation Time:** 5 min. **Cooking Time:** 10 min.

INGREDIENTS

- 8 slices of bacon
- 8 large eggs
- Salt and pepper to taste

DIRECTIONS:

Preheat the air fryer to 400°F. Arrange bacon slices in a single layer in the air fryer basket. Cook for 5-7 minutes until crispy. Remove and set aside on a paper towel to drain.

Crack the eggs directly into the air fryer basket or use silicone cups. Cook for 4-5 minutes until the whites are set, but the yolks are still runny.

Season the eggs with salt and pepper. Serve the crispy bacon alongside the eggs.

Nutritional Information (Approximate per serving):
Calories: 300, Protein: 20g, Fat: 25g, Carbs: 1g

2. Pork Sausage

Servings: 4 **Preparation Time:** 10 min. **Cooking Time:** 10 min.

INGREDIENTS

- 1 lb ground pork
- 1 tsp salt
- 1/2 tsp black pepper, garlic powder
- 1/2 tsp onion powder, paprika

DIRECTIONS:

Preheat the air fryer to 375°F.

In a bowl, combine ground pork with salt, pepper, garlic powder, onion powder, and paprika. Form the mixture into 8 sausages.

Place the sausages in a single layer in the air fryer basket. Cook 7-8 minutes on each side until the sausage is fully cooked and golden brown.

Nutritional Information (Approximate per serving):
Calories: 250, Protein: 18g, Fat: 20g, Carbs: 1g

3. Beef Steak and Eggs

Servings: 4   **Preparation Time:** 10 min.   **Cooking Time:** 15 min.

INGREDIENTS

- 4 small beef steaks (sirloin or ribeye)
- 8 large eggs
- Salt and pepper to taste
- 2 tbsp butter

DIRECTIONS:

Preheat the air fryer to 400°F.

Season the steaks with salt and pepper. Place the steaks in the air fryer basket and cook for 8-10 minutes, flipping halfway through. Remove the steaks and let them rest.

Meanwhile, crack the eggs into the air fryer basket. Cook the eggs for 4-5 minutes until the whites are set.

Top each steak with a pat of butter and serve with the eggs.

Nutritional Information (Approximate per serving):
Calories: 450, Protein: 35g, Fat: 35g, Carbs: 1g

4. Ham and Egg Cups

Servings: 4   **Preparation Time:** 10 min.   **Cooking Time:** 10 min.

INGREDIENTS

- 8 slices of deli ham
- 8 large eggs
- Salt and pepper to taste
- 1/4 cup shredded cheese

DIRECTIONS:

Preheat the air fryer to 350°F.

Line the air fryer basket with ham slices, forming cups. Crack an egg into each ham cup. Cook for 8-10 minutes until the eggs are set.

Sprinkle with cheese, if using, and cook for an additional 1-2 minutes until the cheese is melted.

Nutritional Information (Approximate per serving):
Calories: 200, Protein: 18g, Fat: 13g, Carbs: 1g

5. Breakfast Meatballs

Servings: 4 **Preparation Time:** 15 min. **Cooking Time:** 12 min.

INGREDIENTS

- 1 lb ground beef
- 1/2 lb ground pork
- 1 tsp salt
- 1/2 tsp black pepper, garlic powder, onion powder
- 1/4 tsp paprika

DIRECTIONS:

Preheat the air fryer to 375°F.

Combine ground beef, pork, salt, pepper, garlic powder, onion powder, and paprika in a large bowl. Form the mixture into 16 meatballs.

Place the meatballs in a single layer in the air fryer basket. Cook for 10-12 minutes, shaking the basket halfway through to ensure even cooking.

Nutritional Information (Approximate per serving):
Calories: 300, Protein: 25g, Fat: 20g, Carbs: 1g

---

6. Chicken Sausages

Servings: 4 **Preparation Time:** 10 min. **Cooking Time:** 10 min.

INGREDIENTS

- 1 lb ground chicken
- 1 tsp salt
- 1/2 tsp black pepper, paprika
- 1/2 tsp garlic powder, onion powder

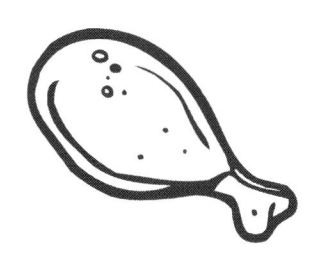

DIRECTIONS:

Preheat the air fryer to 375°F.

Mix ground chicken with salt, pepper, paprika, garlic powder, and onion powder in a bowl.

Form the mixture into 8 sausages. Place the sausages in a single layer in the air fryer basket.

Cook for 7-8 minutes on each side until fully cooked.

Nutritional Information (Approximate per serving):
Calories: 200, Protein: 20g, Fat: 12g, Carbs: 1g

7. Scotch Eggs

Servings: 4 **Preparation Time:** 15 min. **Cooking Time:** 15 min.

INGREDIENTS

- 8 large eggs
- 1 lb ground sausage
- 1 egg (for coating)
- ½ cup breadcrumbs
- Salt and pepper (to taste)

Optional: herbs like parsley or thyme

DIRECTIONS:

Preheat the air fryer to 250°F (120°C) and cook 4 eggs in the air fryer basket for 15-16 minutes.

Once done, transfer the eggs to a bowl of ice water to cool for 5 minutes, then peel and set them aside. Season 1 pound of sausage meat with salt, pepper, and optional herbs, dividing it into 4 portions. Flatten each portion into a disc and wrap it around a boiled egg, making sure the egg is fully enclosed.

Preheat the air fryer to 400°F (200°C).
Beat 1 egg in a bowl and coat each sausage-wrapped egg in the beaten egg, followed by breadcrumbs. Lightly spray or brush the air fryer basket with oil and place the coated Scotch eggs in the basket, ensuring they don't touch. Cook at 400°F (200°C) for 12-15 minutes, turning halfway through, until the sausage is fully cooked and the coating is golden and crispy.

Nutritional Information (Approximate per serving):
Calories: 350, Protein: 25g, Fat: 27g, Carbs: 1g

8. Beef Liver and Egg Scramble

Servings: 4 **Preparation Time:** 5 min. **Cooking Time:** 10 min.

INGREDIENTS

- 1/2 lb beef liver, chopped
- 8 large eggs
- Salt and pepper to taste
- 1 tbsp butter

DIRECTIONS:

Preheat the air fryer to 350°F (175°C).

Place the liver in the air fryer and cook for 6-8 minutes until browned. Remove and set aside.

Whisk the eggs with salt and pepper, pour into an air fryer-safe dish with butter, and cook for 5-6 minutes, stirring halfway through.

Add the cooked liver to the eggs and serve.

Nutritional Information (Approximate per serving):
Calories: 300 , Protein: 27g, Fat: 20g, Carbs: 2g

9. Pork Breakfast Tacos

Servings: 4   **Preparation Time:** 10 min.   **Cooking Time:** 15 min.

INGREDIENTS

- 1 lb ground pork
- 1 tsp salt
- 1/2 tsp black pepper, garlic powder, onion powder
- 8 large eggs
- 1/4 cup shredded cheese

DIRECTIONS:

Preheat the air fryer to 375°F (190°C). Place 1 pound of ground pork in the air fryer basket, breaking it up into crumbles. Cook for 8-10 minutes, stirring halfway through, until fully browned and cooked through. Remove the pork and set aside. Crack and whisk 4 eggs, pour them into a small heatproof dish that fits in your air fryer, and cook at 320°F (160°C) for 5-6 minutes, stirring halfway through, until softly scrambled. Remove the eggs. Assemble the tacos by filling small air-fried egg wraps made from whisked eggs cooked in the air fryer (instead of tortillas) with the cooked pork.

Nutritional Information (Approximate per serving):
Calories: 350, Protein: 25g, Fat: 27g, Carbs: 1g

10. Shrimp and Egg Scramble

Servings: 4   **Preparation Time:** 10 min.   **Cooking Time:** 10 min.

INGREDIENTS

- 1 lb large shrimp, peeled and deveined
- 8 large eggs
- Salt and pepper to taste
- 1/4 tsp paprika, garlic powder

DIRECTIONS:

Preheat the air fryer to 375°F (190°C). Place the peeled and deveined shrimp in the air fryer basket, season with salt, pepper, paprika, and garlic powder, then cook for 6-8 minutes, shaking the basket halfway through until the shrimp are pink and cooked through. While the shrimp cook, crack and whisk 8 large eggs, seasoning with salt and pepper. After the shrimp are done, remove them from the air fryer and set aside. Pour the whisked eggs into a small heatproof dish that fits in your air fryer, then cook at 320°F (160°C) for 5-6 minutes, stirring halfway through, until softly scrambled. Once the eggs are done, mix them with the cooked shrimp and serve immediately.

Nutritional Information (Approximate per serving):
Calories: 250, Protein: 30g, Fat: 10g, Carbs: 1g

11. Cod and Egg Breakfast Bowls

Servings: 4   Preparation Time: 10 min.   Cooking Time: 15 min.

INGREDIENTS

- 1 lb cod fillets
- 8 large eggs
- Salt and pepper to taste
- 1/4 tsp paprika, garlic powder

DIRECTIONS:

Preheat the air fryer to 375°F (190°C). Season the cod fillets with salt, pepper, paprika, and garlic powder, then place them in the air fryer basket. Cook for 10-12 minutes, flipping halfway through, until the cod is flaky and cooked through. While the cod is cooking, crack and whisk 8 large eggs, seasoning with salt and pepper. Once the cod is done, remove it from the air fryer and set aside. Pour the whisked eggs into a small heatproof dish that fits in your air fryer and cook at 320°F (160°C) for 5-6 minutes, stirring halfway through, until softly scrambled.

Nutritional Information (Approximate per serving):
Calories: 250, Protein: 30g, Fat: 10g, Carbs: 1g

12. Bacon and Steak Frittata

Servings: 4   Preparation Time: 10 min.   Cooking Time: 15 min.

INGREDIENTS

- 8 large eggs
- 1/2 lb cooked steak, chopped
- 6 slices of bacon, cooked and chopped
- Salt and pepper to taste

DIRECTIONS:

Preheat the air fryer to 350°F (175°C).

Whisk eggs with salt and pepper. Combine steak and bacon in an air fryer-safe dish.

Pour the eggs over the mixture and cook for 10-12 minutes, until the eggs are set and fully cooked.

Nutritional Information (Approximate per serving):
Calories: 380, Protein: 33g, Fat: 28g, Carbs: 1g

13. Ham and Cheese Breakfast Rolls

🍴 Servings: 4   🍲 Preparation Time: 10 min.   ⏲ Cooking Time: 10 min.

INGREDIENTS

- 8 slices of deli ham
- 8 slices of cheese
- 8 large eggs
- Salt and pepper to taste

DIRECTIONS:

Preheat the air fryer to 375°F.

Roll each slice of ham with a slice of cheese inside. Crack the eggs into a bowl and whisk with salt and pepper. Dip each ham and cheese roll into the egg mixture.

Place the rolls in a single layer in the air fryer basket. Cook for 8-10 minutes until the eggs are set and the cheese is melted.

Nutritional Information (Approximate per serving):
Calories: 250, Protein: 20g, Fat: 18g, Carbs: 1g

14. Carnivore Breakfast Pizza

🍴 Servings: 4   🍲 Preparation Time: 10 min.   ⏲ Cooking Time: 15 min.

INGREDIENTS

- 8 large eggs
- 1/2 lb ground beef
- 1/2 cup shredded cheese
- Salt and pepper to taste

DIRECTIONS:

Preheat the air fryer to 350°F (175°C).

Cook the ground beef in the air fryer for 8-10 minutes, stirring halfway through until browned. Remove and set aside.

Whisk eggs with salt and pepper, pour into an air fryer-safe dish, and cook for 5-6 minutes. Add beef and cheese on top and cook for another 5 minutes until set.

Slice and serve.

Nutritional Information (Approximate per serving):
Calories: 380, Protein: 30g, Fat: 28g, Carbs: 1g

15. Beef and Cheese Omelette

Servings: 4   **Preparation Time:** 10 min.   **Cooking Time:** 20 min.

INGREDIENTS

- 8 large eggs
- 1/2 cup heavy cream
- 1/2 lb ground beef
- 1/2 cup shredded cheese
- Salt and pepper to taste
- 1/4 tsp garlic powder, onion powder

DIRECTIONS:

Preheat the air fryer to 375°F (190°C). Place the ground beef in the air fryer basket, season with salt, pepper, garlic powder, and onion powder, and cook for 8-10 minutes, stirring halfway through, until browned and fully cooked. Remove the beef and set aside. Whisk together the eggs, heavy cream, salt, and pepper in a bowl. Lightly spray a heatproof dish that fits your air fryer with cooking spray. Pour the egg mixture into the dish and evenly sprinkle the cooked ground beef and shredded cheese. Lower the air fryer temperature to 320°F (160°C) and cook the omelette for 8-10 minutes, until the eggs are set and the cheese is melted.

Nutritional Information (Approximate per serving):
Calories: 300, Protein: 20g, Fat: 25g, Carbs: 2g

16. Shrimp and Bacon Skewers

Servings: 4   **Preparation Time:** 15 min.   **Cooking Time:** 10 min.

INGREDIENTS

- 1 lb large shrimp, peeled and deveined
- 8 slices of bacon
- Salt and pepper to taste
- 1/4 tsp garlic powder
- Wooden skewers

DIRECTIONS:

Preheat the air fryer to 400°F.

Cut each bacon slice in half. Wrap each shrimp with a half slice of bacon and secure with a wooden skewer. Season with salt, pepper, and garlic powder.

Place the skewers in a single layer in the air fryer basket. Cook for 8-10 minutes until the bacon is crispy and the shrimp are cooked.

Nutritional Information (Approximate per serving):
Calories: 250, Protein: 25g, Fat: 15g, Carbs: 1g

17. Chicken Heart and Egg Skewers

Servings: 4 **Preparation Time:** 10 min. **Cooking Time:** 20 min.

INGREDIENTS

- 1 lb chicken hearts
- 8 large eggs
- 1 tbsp olive oil
- Salt and pepper to taste
- 1/4 tsp garlic powder

DIRECTIONS:

Preheat the air fryer to 375°F (190°C).

Toss the chicken hearts with olive oil, salt, pepper, and garlic powder. Thread the hearts onto skewers. Place in the air fryer basket and cook for 8-10 minutes, flipping halfway through until the hearts are crispy on the edges.

Meanwhile, place the eggs in ramekins or an air fryer-safe dish. Cook in the air fryer at 320°F (160°C) for 6-8 minutes until the eggs are soft-set.

Serve the chicken hearts with the eggs.

Nutritional Information (Approximate per serving):
Calories: 350, Protein: 35g, Fat: 20g, Carbs: 1g

18. Turkey Heart and Scallop Scramble

Servings: 4 **Preparation Time:** 10 min. **Cooking Time:** 20 min.

INGREDIENTS

- 1/2 lb turkey hearts, cubed
- 1/2 lb scallops
- 8 large eggs
- 1 tbsp butter, melted
- Salt and pepper to taste

DIRECTIONS:

Preheat the air fryer to 400°F (200°C).

Toss the turkey hearts and scallops with melted butter, salt, and pepper. Place them in the air fryer basket and cook for 8-10 minutes, shaking the basket halfway through.

While the hearts and scallops cook, whisk the eggs with salt and pepper and cook in an air fryer-safe dish at 320°F (160°C) for 6-8 minutes, stirring halfway through.

Serve scrambled eggs with turkey hearts and scallops.

Nutritional Information (Approximate per serving):
Calories: 380 l, Protein: 40g, Fat: 22g, Carbs: 1g

CHAPTER 9

POULTRY, TURKEY & DUCK

19. Seasoned Chicken Drumsticks 40
20. Chicken Thighs 40
21. Turkey Breast 41
22. Chicken Roulade 41
23. Smoked Chicken 42
24. Turkey Bacon Medallions............................. 42
25. Quail with Herb Butter 43
26. Turkey Turrets 43
27. Crispy Duck Breast 44

28. Cutlets Stuffed with Bacon & Cheese 44
29. Chicken Soufflé 45
30. Turkey Muffins 45
31. Parmesan Baked Duck................................. 46
32. Chicken Cutlets with Cottage Cheese......... 46
33. Turkey and Cheese Pie................................ 47
34. Smoked Turkey Legs 47
35. Chicken Legs Wrapped in Bacon 48
36. Creamy Chicken Breast............................... 48

19. Seasoned Chicken Drumsticks

Servings: 4 **Preparation Time:** 5 min. **Cooking Time:** 30 min.

INGREDIENTS

- 8 chicken drumsticks
- Salt & Black pepper to taste
- 2 tbsp butter, melted (for brushing)

DIRECTIONS:

Pat the chicken drumsticks dry with paper towels. This helps the skin get crispy. Season the drumsticks generously with salt and black pepper.

Preheat the air fryer to 380°F (193°C).

Brush the drumsticks with melted butter to help the seasoning adhere and to add flavor. Arrange the drumsticks in the air fryer basket, ensuring they are not touching for even cooking.

Cook for 15 minutes, then flip the drumsticks and cook for 15 minutes.

Nutritional Information (per serving):
Calories: 290, Protein: 24g, Fat: 22g, Carbs: 0g

20. Chicken Thighs

Servings: 4 **Preparation Time:** 10 min. **Cooking Time:** 25 min.

INGREDIENTS

- 8 bone-in, skin-on chicken thighs
- 2 tbsp olive oil
- 1 tsp salt
- 1/2 tsp black pepper
- 1 tsp garlic powder, paprika

DIRECTIONS:

Preheat the air fryer to 375°F.

Rub the chicken thighs with olive oil. Season with salt, pepper, garlic powder, and paprika. Place the chicken thighs in a single layer in the air fryer basket.

Cook for 25 minutes, flipping halfway through, until the skin is crispy.

Nutritional Information (Approximate per serving):
Calories: 400, Protein: 30g, Fat: 30g, Carbs: 1g

21. Turkey Breast

🍴 Servings: 4   🍲 Preparation Time: 10 min.   ⏲ Cooking Time: 30 min.

INGREDIENTS

- 2 lbs turkey breast, boneless and skinless
- 2 tbsp olive oil
- 1 tsp salt
- 1/2 tsp black pepper
- 1 tsp garlic powder, dried thyme

DIRECTIONS:

Preheat the air fryer to 350°F.

Rub the turkey breast with olive oil. Season with salt, pepper, garlic powder, and dried thyme. Place the turkey breast in the air fryer basket.

Cook for 30 minutes, flipping halfway through.

Nutritional Information (Approximate per serving):
Calories: 280, Protein: 50g, Fat: 8g, Carbs: 1g

22. Chicken Roulade

🍴 Servings: 4   🍲 Preparation Time: 20 min.   ⏲ Cooking Time: 25 min.

INGREDIENTS

- 4 large, boneless, skinless chicken breasts
- 8 slices of prosciutto
- 4 slices of cheese
- 2 tbsp olive oil
- 1 tsp salt
- 1/2 tsp black pepper, garlic powder, paprika
- Toothpicks or kitchen twine

DIRECTIONS:

Place each chicken breast between two sheets of plastic wrap. Using a meat mallet, gently pound the chicken to an even thickness, about 1/4 inch. Lay two slices of prosciutto on each flattened chicken breast. Place a slice of cheese on top of the prosciutto. Roll up each chicken breast tightly, starting from the narrower end, and secure it with toothpicks or kitchen twine. Rub the outside of each roulade with olive oil—season with salt, pepper, garlic powder, and paprika.

Preheat your air fryer to 375°F (190°C).

Place the chicken roulades in the air fryer basket, seam side down. Cook for 20-25 minutes, turning halfway through, until the chicken is cooked through and golden brown.

Nutritional Information (Approximate per serving):
Calories: 350, Protein: 45g, Fat: 18g, Carbs: 1g

23. Smoked Chicken

Servings: 4　　**Preparation Time:** 15 min.　　**Cooking Time:** 45 min.

INGREDIENTS

- 1 whole chicken (about 3-4 lbs)
- 2 tbsp olive oil
- 1 tbsp smoked paprika, salt
- 1/2 tsp black pepper, garlic powder, onion powder, dried thyme
- 1/2 tsp dried rosemary, dried oregano

DIRECTIONS:

Simply rinse it under cold water and pat dry with paper towels. Mix the olive oil, smoked paprika, salt, pepper, garlic powder, onion powder, thyme, rosemary, and oregano in a small bowl. Rub the seasoning mixture all over the chicken, getting under the skin and inside the cavity for maximum flavor.

Preheat your air fryer to 360°F (182°C).

Place the seasoned chicken in the air fryer basket, breast side down. Cook for 25 minutes, then carefully flip the chicken breast side up. Continue cooking for 20 minutes.

Nutritional Information (Approximate per serving):
Calories: 400, Protein: 35g, Fat: 28g, Carbs: 2g

24. Turkey Bacon Medallions

Servings: 4　　**Preparation Time:** 15 min.　　**Cooking Time:** 20 min.

INGREDIENTS

- 4 turkey tenderloin medallions (about 6 oz each)
- 8 slices of turkey bacon
- 1 tbsp olive oil
- 1 tsp salt
- 1/2 tsp black pepper, garlic powder, onion powder
- Toothpicks

DIRECTIONS:

Preheat the air fryer to 375°F (190°C).

Pat the turkey medallions dry with paper towels. Rub each medallion with olive oil. Mix the salt, pepper, garlic, and onion powder in a small bowl. Sprinkle the seasoning mixture evenly over both sides of the turkey medallions. Wrap each turkey medallion with two slices of turkey bacon, securing the ends with toothpicks. Ensure the bacon is snug but not too tight to avoid squeezing the juices out of the meat during cooking. Place the bacon-wrapped medallions in the air fryer basket in a single layer, ensuring they do not touch each other for even cooking. Cook for 10 minutes on one side, then flip and cook for 8-10 minutes.

Nutritional Information (Approximate per serving):
Calories: 300, Protein: 40g, Fat: 15g, Carbs: 2g

25. Quail with Herb Butter

🍴 Servings: 4   🍲 Preparation Time: 15 min.   ⭘ Cooking Time: 25 min.

INGREDIENTS

- 4 whole quails
- 4 tbsp unsalted butter, softened
- 1 tbsp fresh rosemary, fresh thyme, fresh parsley, finely chopped
- 1 tsp salt, olive oil
- 1/2 tsp black pepper

DIRECTIONS:

Combine the softened butter, rosemary, thyme, parsley, salt, and black pepper in a small bowl. Preheat the air fryer to 375°F (190°C). Pat the quails dry with paper towels. Carefully loosen the skin of each quail by gently sliding your fingers under the skin, being careful not to tear it. Divide the herb butter mixture into four portions and spread it evenly under the skin of each quail, ensuring that the meat is well coated with the butter. Rub the outside of the quails with olive oil. Season the quails with additional salt and pepper if desired. Place the quails in the air fryer basket, breast side up, ensuring they are not touching each other for even cooking. Cook for 15 minutes, then carefully flip the quails and cook for 10 minutes.

Nutritional Information (Approximate per serving):
Calories: 350, Protein: 28g, Fat: 25g, Carbs: 1g

26. Turkey Turrets

🍴 Servings: 4   🍲 Preparation Time: 15 min.   ⭘ Cooking Time: 20 min.

INGREDIENTS

- 1 lb ground turkey
- 1/2 cup grated Parmesan cheese
- 2 cloves garlic, minced
- 1 large egg
- 1 tsp salt
- 1/2 tsp black pepper, dried oregano, dried basil
- 2 tbsp olive oil

DIRECTIONS:

In a large bowl, combine the ground turkey, grated Parmesan cheese, minced garlic, egg, salt, pepper, oregano, and basil. Mix well until all ingredients are thoroughly combined. Using your hands or a meatball scoop, form the mixture into small, evenly-sized meatballs (about 1.5 inches in diameter).

Preheat your air fryer to 375°F (190°C). Brush the meatballs lightly with olive oil to ensure they crisp up nicely. Place the meatballs in a single layer in the air fryer basket, ensuring they do not touch each other for even cooking. Cook for 10 minutes, then gently shake the basket or turn the meatballs to ensure even cooking. Continue cooking for an additional 8-10 minutes

Nutritional Information (per serving):
Calories: 280, Protein: 30g, Fat: 15g, Carbs: 2g

27. Crispy Duck Breast

Servings: 4 **Preparation Time:** 15 min. **Cooking Time:** 45 min.

INGREDIENTS

- 4 duck breasts
- 1/2 tsp black pepper
- 1 tsp salt, garlic powder, onion powder, dried thyme
- 1 tbsp olive oil

DIRECTIONS:

This recipe is simple and straightforward. Preheat the air fryer to 375°F (190°C). Pat the duck breasts dry with paper towels. Score the skin of the duck breasts in a crisscross pattern, being careful not to cut into the meat. Mix, black pepper, garlic powder, onion powder, and dried thyme. Rub the in a small bowl seasoning mixture evenly over both sides of the duck breasts. Drizzle the olive oil over the duck breasts and rub it in to ensure an even coating. Place the duck breasts in the air fryer basket, skin side down. Cook for 25 minutes. Flip the duck breasts and cook for 20 minutes.

Nutritional Information (Approximate per serving):
Calories: 400, Protein: 30g, Fat: 30g, Carbs: 1g

28. Cutlets Stuffed with Bacon and Cheese

Servings: 4 **Preparation Time:** 20 min. **Cooking Time:** 25 min.

INGREDIENTS

- 4 large turkey cutlets (about 6 oz each)
- 8 slices of bacon
- 1/2 cup shredded cheese (cheddar, mozzarella, or your choice)
- 2 tbsp olive oil
- 1 tsp salt
- 1/2 tsp black pepper, garlic powder, onion powder
- Toothpicks

DIRECTIONS:

Preheat the air fryer to 375°F (190°C).

Pound the turkey cutlets to 1/4 inch thickness using a meat mallet. Lay the cutlets flat, add bacon and cheese on top, then roll tightly and secure with toothpicks.

Rub with olive oil and season with salt, pepper, garlic, and onion powder. Place the turkey rolls in the air fryer basket, ensuring they don't touch.

Cook for 15 minutes, flip, and cook for an additional 10 minutes.

Nutritional Information (Approximate per serving):
Calories: 400, Protein: 42g, Fat: 22g, Carbs: 2g

29. Chicken Soufflé

🍴 Servings: 4　　🍲 Preparation Time: 20 min.　　⭕ Cooking Time: 25 min.

INGREDIENTS

- 2 large chicken breasts (about 1 lb), cooked and shredded
- 4 large eggs, separated
- 1/2 cup heavy cream, shredded cheese
- 1/4 cup grated Parmesan cheese
- 1/2 tsp salt
- 1/4 tsp black pepper, garlic powder, onion powder
- 1 tbsp butter for

DIRECTIONS:

Preheat the air fryer to 350°F (175°C).

Combine the shredded chicken, egg yolks, heavy cream, shredded cheese, Parmesan cheese, salt, pepper, garlic powder, and onion powder in a large bowl. Mix well until all ingredients are thoroughly combined. In a separate bowl, beat the egg whites until stiff peaks form. Gently fold the beaten egg whites into the chicken mixture, careful not to deflate the egg whites. Grease an air fryer-safe baking dish or soufflé dish with butter. Pour the mixture into the prepared dish and smooth the top.

Place the dish in the air fryer basket and cook for 20-25 minutes or until the soufflé is puffed and golden brown.

Nutritional Information (Approximate per serving):
Calories: 300, Protein: 30g, Fat: 18g, Carbs: 2g

30. Turkey Muffins

🍴 Servings: 4　　🍲 Preparation Time: 15 min.　　⭕ Cooking Time: 20 min.

INGREDIENTS

- 1 lb ground turkey
- 1/2 cup grated Parmesan cheese
- 1 large egg
- 1 tsp salt
- 1/2 tsp black pepper, dried oregano, dried basil
- 1 tbsp olive oil

DIRECTIONS:

Preheat the air fryer to 375°F (190°C).

In a large bowl, combine the ground turkey, grated Parmesan cheese, egg, salt, pepper, oregano, and basil. Mix well until all ingredients are thoroughly combined. Grease a silicone muffin tray or air fryer-safe muffin cups with olive oil. Divide the turkey mixture evenly among the muffin cups, pressing the mixture down lightly.

Place the muffin tray or cups in the air fryer basket. Cook for 20-25 minutes until the muffins are golden brown.

Nutritional Information (per serving):
Calories: 250, Protein: 25g, Fat: 15g, Carbs: 2g

31. Parmesan Baked Duck

🍴 Servings: 4　　🍲 Preparation Time: 20 min.　　⭕ Cooking Time: 40 min.

INGREDIENTS

- 4 duck breasts
- 1/2 cup grated Parmesan cheese
- 1 tbsp fresh rosemary, fresh thyme, finely chopped
- 1 tsp salt
- 1/2 tsp black pepper, garlic powder, onion powder
- 2 tbsp olive oil

DIRECTIONS:

Preheat the air fryer to 375°F (190°C). Pat the duck breasts dry with paper towels. Score the skin of the duck breasts in a crisscross pattern, being careful not to cut into the meat. In a small bowl, mix the salt, black pepper, garlic powder, and onion powder. Rub the seasoning mixture evenly over both sides of the duck breasts. Drizzle the olive oil over the duck breasts and rub it in to ensure an even coating. Combine the grated Parmesan cheese, rosemary, and thyme in a separate bowl. Press the Parmesan mixture onto the skin side of each duck breast, ensuring it sticks well. Place the duck breasts in the air fryer basket, skin side up, ensuring they are not touching each other for even cooking. Cook for 30-40 minutes.

Nutritional Information (Approximate per serving):
Calories: 450, Protein: 35g, Fat: 30g, Carbs: 2g

32. Chicken Cutlets with Cottage Cheese

🍴 Servings: 4　　🍲 Preparation Time: 20 min.　　⭕ Cooking Time: 25 min.

INGREDIENTS

- 1 lb ground chicken
- 1/2 cup cottage cheese
- 1/4 cup grated Parmesan cheese
- 1 large egg
- 1 tsp salt
- 1/2 tsp black pepper, dried oregano, dried basil
- 1 tbsp olive oil

DIRECTIONS:

Preheat the air fryer to 375°F (190°C).

In a large bowl, combine the ground chicken, cottage cheese, grated Parmesan cheese, egg, salt, pepper, oregano, and basil. Mix well until all ingredients are thoroughly combined. Divide the mixture into 8 equal portions and shape them into cutlets. Brush the cutlets lightly with olive oil to ensure they crisp up nicely.

Place the cutlets in a single layer in the air fryer basket, ensuring they do not touch each other for even cooking.

Cook for 12 minutes on one side, then flip and cook for 10-13 minutes.

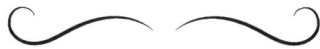

Nutritional Information (Approximate per serving):
Calories: 250, Protein: 30g, Fat: 12g, Carbs: 2g

33. Turkey and Cheese Pie

Servings: 4　　**Preparation Time:** 20 min.　　**Cooking Time:** 30 min.

INGREDIENTS

- 1 lb ground turkey
- 1 cup shredded cheese
- 1/2 cup grated Parmesan cheese
- 1 large egg
- 1 tsp salt
- 1/2 tsp black pepper, dried oregano, dried basil
- 1 tbsp olive oil

DIRECTIONS:

Preheat the air fryer to 375°F (190°C).

In a large bowl, combine the ground turkey, shredded cheese, grated Parmesan cheese, egg, salt, pepper, oregano, and basil. Mix well until all ingredients are thoroughly combined.

Grease an air fryer-safe baking dish with olive oil. Press the turkey mixture into the dish, spreading it evenly to form a pie.

Place the baking dish in the air fryer basket. Cook for 30 minutes.

Nutritional Information (Approximate per serving):
Calories: 350, Protein: 35g, Fat: 20g, Carbs: 3g

34. Smoked Turkey Legs

Servings: 4　　**Preparation Time:** 15 min.　　**Cooking Time:** 40 min.

INGREDIENTS

- 4 turkey legs
- 2 tbsp olive oil
- 1 tbsp smoked paprika
- 1 tsp salt
- 1/2 tsp black pepper, garlic powder, onion powder, dried thyme, dried rosemary

DIRECTIONS:

Preheat the air fryer to 375°F (190°C).

Pat the turkey legs dry with paper towels. Rub each turkey leg with olive oil to ensure the seasoning sticks and the skin crisps up nicely. Mix the smoked paprika, salt, black pepper, garlic powder, onion powder, thyme, and rosemary in a small bowl. Rub the seasoning mixture evenly over all sides of the turkey legs.

Place the seasoned turkey legs in the air fryer basket, ensuring they do not touch each other even when cooking. Cook for 20 minutes, then flip the turkey legs and cook for 20 minutes.

Nutritional Information (per serving):
Calories: 450, Protein: 40g, Fat: 30g, Carbs: 2g

35. Chicken Legs Wrapped in Bacon

🍴 Servings: 4   🍲 Preparation Time: 15 min.   ⭕ Cooking Time: 25 min.

INGREDIENTS

- 8 chicken legs
- 8 slices of bacon
- 1 tbsp olive oil
- 1 tsp salt
- 1/2 tsp black pepper, garlic powder, onion powder, paprika

DIRECTIONS:

Preheat the air fryer to 375°F (190°C). Pat the chicken legs dry with paper towels. Rub each chicken leg with olive oil to ensure the seasoning sticks and the skin crisps up nicely. Mix the salt, black pepper, garlic powder, onion powder, and paprika in a small bowl. Rub the seasoning mixture evenly over all sides of the chicken legs. Wrap each seasoned chicken leg with a slice of bacon, securing the ends with toothpicks if necessary. Place the bacon-wrapped chicken legs in the air fryer basket, ensuring they do not touch each other for even cooking. Cook for 15 minutes, then flip the chicken legs and cook for 10 minutes.

Nutritional Information (Approximate per serving):
Calories: 400 ,Protein: 35g, Fat: 28g, Carbs: 1g

36. Creamy Chicken Breast

🍴 Servings: 4   🍲 Preparation Time: 15 min.   ⭕ Cooking Time: 45 min.

INGREDIENTS

- 4 boneless, skinless chicken breasts
- 1 cup heavy cream
- 1/2 cup grated Parmesan
- 1/4 cup chicken broth
- 1 tbsp olive oil
- 1 tsp salt
- 1/2 tsp black pepper, garlic powder, onion powder

DIRECTIONS:

Preheat the air fryer to 375°F (190°C).
Rub the chicken breasts with olive oil, salt, pepper, garlic powder, and onion powder. Place the chicken breasts in the air fryer basket and cook for 20 minutes, flipping halfway through. While the chicken is cooking, mix the heavy cream, Parmesan cheese, and chicken broth in an air fryer-safe dish. After 20 minutes, remove the chicken from the basket and pour the cream mixture over the chicken.
Return the chicken and the dish to the air fryer, cooking for 5 minutes until the sauce is bubbly and the chicken is cooked through.

Nutritional Information (Approximate per serving):
Calories: 450, Protein: 40g, Fat: 30g, Carbs: 3g

CHAPTER 10

BEEF, LAMB, PORK, ETC

37. Pork Chops with Herb Crust 50
38. Rack of Lamb 50
39. Lamb and Feta Patties 51
40. Lamb Kebab 51
41. Glazed Ribs 52
42. Ribeye Steak 52
43. Carnivore Burger 53
44. Ground Pork Frittata 54
45. T-Bone Steak 54
46. Bone-in Pork Cutlets 55
47. Elk Steak 55
48. Filet Mignon 56

49. New York Strip Steak 56
50. Bison Meatloaf 57
51. Bacon-Wrapped Pork Tenderloin 57
52. Braised Rabbit Pie 58
53. Whiskey Marinated Beef 59
54. Escalope of Lamb 60
55. Beef Steaks in Hot Sauce 60
56. Breaded Pork Steak 61
57. Meatloaf 62
58. Beef with Egg Butter Sauce 63
59. Bison Blue Cheese Burgers 64

37. Pork Chops with Herb Crust

Servings: 4   **Preparation Time:** 10 min.   **Cooking Time:** 15 min.

INGREDIENTS

- 4 pork chops, bone-in, 1-inch thick
- 4 tbsp butter, melted
- Salt and black pepper to taste
- 1 tsp garlic powder, dried thyme, dried rosemary

DIRECTIONS:

Preheat your air fryer to 380°F (193°C).

Pat the pork chops dry with a paper towel. Mix the melted butter with garlic powder, thyme, and rosemary in a small bowl—season both sides of the pork chops with salt and black pepper.

Brush the herb butter mixture onto both sides of each pork chop. Place pork chops in the air fryer basket, ensuring they do not overlap.

Cook for 12 to 15 min., flipping halfway through.

Nutritional Information (Approximate per serving):
Calories: 380, Protein: 35g, Fat: 26g, Carbs: 0g

38. Rack of Lamb

Servings: 4   **Preparation Time:** 10 min.   **Cooking Time:** 20 min

INGREDIENTS

- 1 rack of lamb (about 1.5 to 2 pounds, 8 ribs)
- Salt and black pepper to taste
- 2 tbsp butter, softened

DIRECTIONS:

Let the rack of lamb rest at room temperature for about 30 min. before cooking. Season it generously with salt and black pepper. Rub the rack all over with softened butter.

Optionally, press crushed fresh herbs onto the meat for added flavor.

Preheat the air fryer to 380°F (193°C).

Place the rack of lamb in the air fryer basket, bone side down, so the meaty part is exposed to the heat.

Cook for about 18-20 min. for medium-rare, or adjust the time depending on your preferred level of doneness.

Nutritional Information (Approximate per serving):
Calories: 320, Protein: 25g, Fat: 24g, Carbs: 0g

39. Lamb and Feta Patties

Servings: 4 **Preparation Time:** 15 min. **Cooking Time:** 12 min.

INGREDIENTS

- 1 lb ground lamb
- 1/2 cup crumbled feta cheese
- 1 large egg
- 1/2 tsp salt, black pepper, dried oregano, garlic powder
- 1 tbsp olive oil

DIRECTIONS:

Preheat the air fryer to 375°F (190°C). Combine the ground lamb, feta cheese, egg, salt, pepper, oregano, and garlic powder in a large bowl. Mix well until the ingredients are thoroughly combined. Shape the mixture into 8 equal-sized patties. Lightly brush the air fryer basket with olive oil to prevent sticking, then place the lamb patties in the basket in a single layer. Cook for 10-12 min., flipping halfway through, until the patties are golden brown and cooked through (internal temperature of 160°F).

Nutritional Information (Approximate per serving):
Calories: 320, Protein: 22g, Fat: 25g, Carbs: 1g

40. Lamb Kebab

Servings: 4 **Preparation Time:** 20 min. **Cooking Time:** 15 min.

INGREDIENTS

- 1.5 lbs ground lamb
- 1 large egg
- 1 tsp salt
- 1 tsp ground cumin, ground coriander
- 1/2 tsp black pepper, ground cinnamon, dried oregano dried thyme,
- 1 tbsp olive oil

DIRECTIONS:

Preheat your air fryer to 375°F (190°C).
Combine the ground lamb, egg, salt, black pepper, ground cumin, coriander, cinnamon, oregano, and thyme in a large bowl. Mix well until all ingredients are thoroughly combined. Divide the mixture into 8 equal portions and shape them into long, cylindrical kebabs. Brush the kebabs lightly with olive oil.

Place the kebabs in the air fryer basket in a single layer, ensuring they do not touch each other for even cooking.

Cook for 12-15 min., flipping halfway through, until the kebabs are golden brown and cooked.

Nutritional Information (Approximate per serving):
Calories: 450, Protein: 35g, Fat: 32g, Carbs: 3g

41. Glazed Ribs

Servings: 4   **Preparation Time:** 15 min.   **Cooking Time:** 45 min.

INGREDIENTS

- 2 lbs pork ribs, cut into individual ribs
- 1 tbsp olive oil
- 1 tsp salt
- 1/2 tsp black pepper
- 1 tsp garlic powder, onion powder, smoked paprika
- 1/2 cup sugar-free BBQ sauce

DIRECTIONS:

Preheat your air fryer to 375°F (190°C).

Pat the ribs dry with paper towels. Rub the ribs with olive oil to ensure even cooking. Mix the salt, black pepper, garlic powder, onion powder, and smoked paprika in a small bowl. Rub the seasoning mixture evenly over the ribs.

Place the seasoned ribs in the air fryer basket in a single layer. Cook for 30 min., flipping halfway through. If using BBQ sauce, brush the ribs with the sauce after 30 minutes of cooking. Cook for 10-15 min. until the ribs are tender.

Nutritional Information (Approximate per serving):
Calories: 450, Protein: 35g, Fat: 32g, Carbs: 3g

42. Ribeye Steak

Servings: 4   **Preparation Time:** 5 min.   **Cooking Time:** 15 min.

INGREDIENTS

- 4 ribeye steaks
- 2 tbsp olive oil
- 1 tsp salt
- 1/2 tsp black pepper, garlic powder

DIRECTIONS:

Preheat your air fryer to 400°F (200°C).

Rub the steaks with olive oil and season with salt, black pepper, and garlic powder.

Place the steaks in the air fryer basket in a single layer. Cook for 10-12 minutes for medium-rare, flipping halfway through.

Nutritional Information (Approximate per serving):
Calories: 500, Protein: 45g, Fat: 35g, Carbs: 1g

43. Carnivore Burger

Servings: 4 **Preparation Time:** 10 min. **Cooking Time:** 25 min.

INGREDIENTS

- 1 lb ground beef
- 1/2 lb ground pork
- 4 slices of cheddar
- 8 slices of bacon
- 1 tsp salt
- 1/2 tsp black pepper, garlic powder, onion powder
- 1 tbsp olive oil

DIRECTIONS:

Preheat your air fryer to 375°F (190°C).

In a large bowl, combine the ground beef and ground pork. Add the salt, black pepper, garlic powder, and onion powder. Divide the mixture into four equal portions and shape them into patties.

Place the bacon slices in the air fryer basket in a single layer. Cook for 8-10 min. or until crispy. Remove the bacon from the air fryer and set aside. Brush the burger patties lightly with olive oil. Place the patties in the air fryer basket in a single layer. Cook for 10-12 min., flipping halfway through, until the internal temperature reaches 160°F (71°C).

During the last 2 min. of cooking, place a slice of cheese on each patty to melt. Next, wrap each cheese patty in bacon.

Nutritional Information (Approximate per serving):
Calories: 600, Protein: 40g, Fat: 50g, Carbs: 1g

44. Ground Pork Frittata

🍴 Servings: 4   🍲 Preparation Time: 15 min.   ⏲ Cooking Time: 25 min.

INGREDIENTS

- 1 lb ground pork
- 8 large eggs
- 1/2 cup heavy cream, grated Parmesan
- 1/4 cup finely chopped onions
- 2 cloves garlic, minced
- 1 tsp salt
- 1/2 tsp black pepper, garlic powder, onion powder
- 1 tbsp olive oil

DIRECTIONS:

Preheat the air fryer to 375°F (190°C).

Heat the olive oil in an air fryer-safe dish for 1-2 min.. Add the ground pork, chopped onions, minced garlic, salt, pepper, garlic powder, and onion powder. Cook for 8-10 min., stirring halfway through until the pork is browned and cooked through. Whisk the eggs, heavy cream, and Parmesan cheese in a separate bowl.

Once the pork is cooked, pour the egg mixture in the same air fryer-safe dish. Return the dish to the air fryer and reduce the temperature to 350°F (175°C).

Cook for 10-12 min. or until the frittata is set and golden.

Nutritional Information (Approximate per serving):
Calories: 400, Protein: 25g, Fat: 30g, Carbs: 3g

45. T-Bone Steak

🍴 Servings: 4   🍲 Preparation Time: 5 min.   ⏲ Cooking Time: 10 min.

INGREDIENTS

- 4 T-bone steaks
- 2 tbsp olive oil
- 1/2 tsp black pepper
- 1 tsp salt, garlic powder

DIRECTIONS:

Preheat your air fryer to 400°F (200°C).

Rub the steaks with olive oil and season both sides with salt, black pepper, and garlic powder. Place the steaks in the air fryer basket in a single layer. Cook for 8 min. on each side for medium-rare. Adjust the cooking time to your desired level of doneness.

Remove the steaks from the air fryer and let them rest for 5 min. before serving to allow the juices to redistribute.

Nutritional Information (Approximate per serving):
Calories: 550, Protein: 48g, Fat: 38g, Carbs: 1g

46. Bone-in Pork Cutlets

Servings: 4 **Preparation Time:** 15 min **Cooking Time:** 20 min.

INGREDIENTS

- 4 bone-in pork cutlets (about 6-8 oz each)
- 2 tbsp olive oil
- 1 tsp salt
- 1/2 tsp black pepper
- 1 tsp garlic powder, onion powder, smoked paprika
- 1/2 cup grated Parmesan

DIRECTIONS:

Preheat your air fryer to 375°F (190°C) for about 5 min..

Pat the pork cutlets dry with paper towels. Rub each cutlet with olive oil. In a small bowl, mix salt, black pepper, garlic powder, onion powder, and smoked paprika. Season both sides of the cutlets with the spice mixture. Sprinkle Parmesan evenly over both sides of the cutlets, pressing gently to adhere.

Place the cutlets in the air fryer basket in a single layer. Cook for 10 min. on one side, then flip and cook for another 8-10 min .

Nutritional Information (Approximate per serving):
Calories: 420, Protein: 35g, Fat: 28g, Carbs: 2g

47. Elk Steak

Servings: 4 **Preparation Time:** 10 min. **Cooking Time:** 15 min.

INGREDIENTS

- 4 elk steaks (6-8 oz each)
- 1 tbsp olive oil
- 2 cloves garlic, minced
- 1 tsp smoked paprika
- ½ tsp salt
- ½ tsp black pepper

DIRECTIONS:

Preheat your air fryer to 400°F.

In a small bowl, mix olive oil, garlic, smoked paprika, salt, and pepper. Rub the mixture all over the elk steaks. Place the steaks in the air fryer basket without overlapping.

Cook for 6-8 minutes on each side or until the internal temperature reaches 130°F for medium-rare.

Let the steaks rest for 5 minutes before serving.

Nutritional Information (Approximate per serving):
Calories: 220 , Protein: 32g , Fat: 9g , Carbs: 1g

48. Filet Mignon

Servings: 4　　**Preparation Time:** 5 min.　　**Cooking Time:** 12 min.

INGREDIENTS

- 4 filet mignon steaks
- 2 tbsp olive oil
- 1 tsp salt, dried rosemary
- 1/2 tsp black pepper, garlic powder

DIRECTIONS:

Preheat your air fryer to 400°F (200°C).

Rub the steaks with olive oil—season both sides with salt, black pepper, garlic powder, and dried rosemary. Place the steaks in the air fryer basket in a single layer. Cook for 6-7 min. on each side for medium-rare. Adjust the cooking time to your desired level of doneness.

Remove the steaks from the air fryer and let them rest for 5 min. before serving to allow the juices to redistribute.

Nutritional Information (Approximate per serving):
Calories: 400, Protein: 38g, Fat: 28g, Carbs: 1g

49. New York Strip Steak

Servings: 4　　**Preparation Time:** 5 min.　　**Cooking Time:** 15 min.

INGREDIENTS

- 4 New York strip steaks
- 2 tbsp olive oil
- 1 tsp salt, garlic powder
- 1/2 tsp black pepper

DIRECTIONS:

Preheat your air fryer to 400°F (200°C).

Rub the steaks with olive oil and season both sides with salt, black pepper, and garlic powder. Place the steaks in the air fryer basket in a single layer. Cook for 7-8 min. on each side for medium-rare. Adjust the cooking time to your desired level of doneness.

Remove the steaks from the air fryer and let them rest for 5 min. before serving to allow the juices to redistribute.

Nutritional Information (Approximate per serving):
Calories: 500, Protein: 45g, Fat: 35g, Carbs: 1g

50. Bison Meatloaf

Servings: 4   **Preparation Time:** 20 min.   **Cooking Time:** 40 min.

INGREDIENTS

- 1 lb ground bison
- 1/2 cup grated Parmesan
- 1 large egg
- 1 tsp salt
- 1/2 tsp black pepper, garlic powder
- 1 tbsp olive oil

DIRECTIONS:

Preheat the air fryer to 350°F (175°C).

In a bowl, mix the ground bison, Parmesan cheese, egg, salt, pepper, and garlic powder.

Shape the mixture into a small meatloaf and place it in an air fryer-safe dish.

Drizzle with olive oil and cook for 35-40 min., until the internal temperature reaches 160°F, and the meatloaf is browned on top.

Nutritional Information (Approximate per serving):
Calories: 500, Protein: 35g, Fat: 38g, Carbs: 5g

51. Bacon-Wrapped Pork Tenderloin

Servings: 4   **Preparation Time:** 15 min.   **Cooking Time:** 25 min.

INGREDIENTS

- 1 pork tenderloin (about 1.5 lbs)
- 8 slices of bacon
- 2 tbsp olive oil
- 1 tsp salt
- 1/2 tsp black pepper
- 1 tsp garlic powder, onion powder, dried thyme

DIRECTIONS:

Preheat your air fryer to 375°F (190°C) for about 5 min.

Pat the pork tenderloin dry with paper towels. Rub the tenderloin with olive oil. Season all sides of the pork tenderloin with salt, black pepper, garlic powder, onion powder, and dried thyme.

Lay the bacon slices out on a cutting board, slightly overlapping. Place the seasoned pork tenderloin at one end of the bacon slices and roll it up, wrapping the bacon around the tenderloin.

Secure the bacon with toothpicks if necessary. Place the bacon-wrapped pork tenderloin in the air fryer basket. Cook for 20-25 min., flipping halfway through, until the internal temperature reaches 145°F (63°C) and the bacon is crispy.

Nutritional Information (Approximate per serving):
Calories: 450, Protein: 40g, Fat: 30g, Carbs: 1g

52. Braised Rabbit Pie

Servings: 4 **Preparation Time:** 30 min. **Cooking Time:** 1 hour.

INGREDIENTS

- 2 lbs rabbit meat, boneless and cut into chunks
- 1 cup chicken broth
- 1 cup heavy cream
- 1/2 cup grated Parmesan cheese
- 1/4 cup finely chopped onions
- 2 cloves garlic, minced
- 1 tsp salt
- 1/2 tsp black pepper
- 1/2 tsp dried thyme
- 1/2 tsp dried rosemary
- 1 tbsp olive oil
- 1 large egg, beaten (for egg wash)

DIRECTIONS:

Preheat the air fryer to 375°F (190°C).

Heat the olive oil in an air fryer-safe dish for 1-2 minutes. Add the rabbit chunks, chopped onions, minced garlic, salt, pepper, thyme, and rosemary. Cook for 15 minutes, stirring halfway through, until the rabbit is browned and cooked.

Once the rabbit is browned, add the chicken broth and cook for an additional 20 minutes at 350°F (175°C) to allow the rabbit to braise. Stir in the heavy cream and Parmesan cheese, and cook for another 10 minutes until the sauce thickens.

After thickening the sauce, top the rabbit mixture with a layer of beaten egg for a golden crust. Cook for 10 minutes at 350°F (175°C) until the top is golden and set.

Nutritional Information (Approximate per serving):
Calories: 500, Protein: 35g, Fat: 38g, Carbs: 5g

53. Whiskey Marinated Beef

Servings: 4   **Preparation Time:** 2 hours 20 min   **Cooking Time:** 40 min.

INGREDIENTS

- 2 lbs beef steak
- 1/2 cup whiskey
- 1/4 cup soy sauce (or coconut aminos for a soy-free option)
- 2 tbsp olive oil
- 2 tbsp brown sugar
- 2 cloves garlic, minced
- 1 tsp black pepper
- 1 tsp onion powder
- 1 tsp dried thyme
- 1/2 tsp salt

DIRECTIONS:

Combine whiskey, soy sauce, olive oil, brown sugar, minced garlic, black pepper, onion powder, dried thyme, and salt in a bowl. Mix well.

Place the beef steaks in a large resealable plastic bag or a shallow dish. Pour the marinade over the steaks, ensuring they are well coated. Seal the bag or cover the dish and refrigerate for at least 2 hours, preferably overnight, turning occasionally to ensure even marination.

Preheat your air fryer to 400°F (200°C) for about 5 min..

Remove the beef from the marinade and pat dry with paper towels to remove excess marinade. Allow the meat to room temperature for 15-20 min. before cooking.

Place the steaks in the air fryer basket in a single layer. Cook for 7-8 min. on one side, then flip and cook for another 7-8 min. for medium-rare.

Adjust the cooking time according to your desired level of doneness (10 min. per side for medium, 12 min. for well-done).

Nutritional Information (Approximate per serving):
Calories: 450, Protein: 40g, Fat: 30g, Carbs: 3g

54. Escalope of Lamb

Servings: 4 **Preparation Time:** 10 min. **Cooking Time:** 12 min.

INGREDIENTS

- 4 lamb escalopes (about 5-6 oz each)
- 2 tbsp olive oil
- 1 tsp salt
- 1/2 tsp black pepper
- 1 tsp garlic powder, dried rosemary, dried thyme

DIRECTIONS:

Preheat your air fryer to 400°F (200°C) for about 5 min..

Pat the lamb escalopes dry with paper towels. Rub each escalope with olive oil—season both sides with salt, black pepper, garlic powder, rosemary, and thyme. Place the lamb escalopes in the air fryer basket in a single layer.

Cook for 6 min. on each side until the internal temperature reaches 145°F (63°C) for medium-rare. Adjust the cooking time to your desired level of doneness.

Remove the lamb escalopes from the air fryer and let them rest for 5 min. before serving.

Nutritional Information (Approximate per serving):
Calories: 300, Protein: 28g, Fat: 20g, Carbs: 1g

55. Beef Steaks in Hot Sauce

Servings: 4 **Preparation Time:** 15 min. **Cooking Time:** 15 min.

INGREDIENTS

- 4 beef steaks (such as ribeye or sirloin, about 1 inch thick)
- 2 tbsp olive oil
- 1 tsp salt
- 1/2 tsp black pepper, garlic powder, onion powder
- 1 cup hot sauce
- 2 tbsp butter, melted

DIRECTIONS:

Preheat your air fryer to 400°F (200°C) for about 5 min..

Pat the steaks dry with paper towels to ensure a good sear. Rub each steak with olive oil—season both sides of the steaks with salt, black pepper, garlic powder, and onion powder. Place the steaks in the air fryer basket in a single layer. Cook the steaks on one side for 7-8 min., then flip and cook for another 7-8 min. for medium-rare.

Adjust the cooking time according to your desired level of doneness. Mix the hot sauce and melted butter in a small bowl until well combined.

Nutritional Information (Approximate per serving):
Calories: 480, Protein: 40g, Fat: 35g, Carbs: 2g

56. Breaded Pork Steak

Servings: 4 **Preparation Time:** 15 min. **Cooking Time:** 20 min.

INGREDIENTS

- 4 pork steaks (about 6 oz each)
- 1/2 cup grated Parmesan
- 1 tsp garlic powder, onion powder, smoked paprika
- 1/2 tsp salt, black pepper
- 2 large eggs
- 2 tbsp olive oil

DIRECTIONS:

Preheat your air fryer to 375°F (190°C) for about 5 min.

Combine grated Parmesan, garlic powder, onion powder, smoked paprika, salt, and black pepper in a shallow dish. In another shallow dish, beat the eggs. Pat the pork steaks dry with paper towels. Dip each pork steak into the beaten eggs, allowing any excess to drip off. Dredge the pork steaks in the Parmesan mixture, pressing lightly to adhere. Brush the air fryer basket with olive oil to prevent sticking.

Place the breaded pork steaks in the air fryer basket in a single layer. Cook for 10 min., then flip and cook for another 8-10 min. until golden brown.

Nutritional Information (Approximate per serving):
Calories: 500, Protein: 35g, Fat: 35g, Carbs: 5g

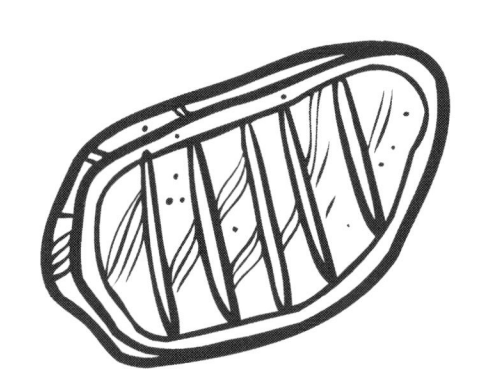

57. Meatloaf

Servings: 4 **Preparation Time: 15 min.** **Cooking Time: 40 min.**

INGREDIENTS

- 1 lb ground beef
- 1/2 lb ground pork
- 1/2 cup grated Parmesan
- 1/4 cup finely chopped onions
- 2 cloves garlic, minced
- 1 large egg
- 1 tsp salt
- 1/2 tsp black pepper, dried thyme, dried oregano, garlic powder, onion powder,
- 2 tbsp tomato paste (optional)

DIRECTIONS:

Preheat your air fryer to 350°F (175°C).

In a large bowl, combine the ground beef, ground pork, Parmesan, onions, garlic, egg, salt, black pepper, thyme, oregano, garlic powder, and onion powder. Mix well until all ingredients are thoroughly combined.

Shape the mixture into a loaf and place it on a piece of parchment paper that fits into your air fryer basket. If desired, spread the tomato paste to the meatloaf for added flavor.

Place the meatloaf in the air fryer basket. Cook for 35-40 min.

Nutritional Information (Approximate per serving):
Calories: 400, Protein: 30g, Fat: 30g, Carbs: 3g

58. Beef with Egg Butter Sauce

🍴 Servings: 4   🍲 Preparation Time: 20 min.   ⏲ Cooking Time: 15 min.

INGREDIENTS

- 4 beef steaks (such as filet mignon or sirloin, about 1 inch thick)
- 2 tbsp olive oil
- 1 tsp salt
- 1/2 tsp black pepper, garlic powder, onion powder

Egg Butter Sauce:

- 4 large eggs
- 1/2 cup unsalted butter
- 1 tbsp lemon juice
- Salt and pepper to taste

DIRECTIONS:

Preheat the air fryer to 400°F (200°C).

Rub the steaks with olive oil, salt, pepper, garlic powder, and onion powder. Place the steaks in the air fryer basket and cook for 10-12 min., flipping halfway through, depending on your desired doneness (medium-rare: 130-135°F). Remove the steaks and let them rest while you prepare the egg butter sauce.

For the Egg Butter Sauce, crack the eggs into an air fryer-safe dish and cook at 320°F (160°C) for 8-10 min., stirring occasionally, until they are fully scrambled.

In a separate air fryer-safe dish, melt the butter at 320°F (160°C) for 2-3 min. until thoroughly melted. Stir in the scrambled eggs and lemon juice into the melted butter.

Season with salt and pepper to taste, and mix until smooth.

Serve the beef steaks hot with the egg butter sauce drizzled over them.

Nutritional Information (Approximate per serving):
Calories: 500, Protein: 42g, Fat: 38g, Carbs: 1 g

59. Bison Blue Cheese Burgers

Servings: 4 **Preparation Time:** 10 min. **Cooking Time:** 12 min.

INGREDIENTS

- 1 lb ground bison
- 4 oz blue cheese crumbles
- 4 slices bacon, cooked and crumbled
- ½ tsp salt
- ½ tsp pepper

DIRECTIONS:

Preheat the air fryer to 375°F (190°C), form the ground bison into 4 patties, season with salt and pepper, place the patties in the air fryer basket and cook for 10 minutes, flipping halfway, top each patty with blue cheese crumbles and cook for an additional 2 minutes, garnish with crumbled bacon before serving.

Nutritional Information (Approximate per serving):
Calories: 450 , Protein: 35g , Fat: 34g , Carbs: 1g

CHAPTER 11

SEAFOOD & FISH

60. Salmon in Sour Cream Sauce 66
61. Fishcakes 66
62. Lobster in Butter Sauce 67
63. Octopus 67
64. Crab Stuffed Squid 68
65. Squid in Sauce 69
66. Zucchini Fritters 69
67. Seafood Stew 70
68. Smoked Crab 71
69. Oyster in Spicy Sauce 71
70. Shrimp in Cheese Sauce 72

71. Cheesy Crusted Salmon 73
72. Ebi Tempura Shrimp 73
73. Mixed Seafood Kebabs 74
74. King Prawn Scampi 74
75. Cream Cheese Salmon Tempura 75
76. Panko Crusted Langoustines 76
77. Scallops in Sour Cream Sauce 76
78. Herbed Baked Pollock 77
79. Mussels with Cheese 77
80. Battered Shrimp Cheese Balls 78

60. Salmon in Sour Cream Sauce

🍴 Servings: 4   🍲 Preparation Time: 5 min.   ⭕ Cooking Time: 10 min.

INGREDIENTS

- 4 salmon fillets (about 6 ounces each)
- Salt and black pepper to taste
- 1 cup sour cream

Optional: herbs such as dill or chives, if permitted on your diet

DIRECTIONS:

Season each salmon fillet with salt and black pepper. Mix the sour cream with optional herbs and add salt and pepper to taste in a small bowl. Adjust the seasoning as necessary. Preheat the air fryer to 400°F (204°C).
Place the salmon fillets in the air fryer basket. Cook for 7 min.. After 7 min., spoon the sour cream sauce over the salmon fillets and continue to cook for an additional 3 min., or until the salmon is cooked through and flakes easily with a fork. Serve the salmon fillets hot, topped with any remaining sour cream sauce.

Nutritional Information (per serving):
Calories: 320, Protein: 23g, Fat: 24g, Carbs: 2g

61. Fishcakes

🍴 Servings: 4   🍲 Preparation Time: 15 min.   ⭕ Cooking Time: 20 min.

INGREDIENTS

- 1 lb white fish fillets (cod, haddock, or tilapia)
- 1/2 cup grated Parmesan
- 1/4 cup finely chopped onions
- 2 cloves garlic, minced
- 1 large egg
- 1 tsp salt
- 1/2 tsp black pepper, paprika
- 2 tbsp olive oil

DIRECTIONS:

Preheat your air fryer to 375°F (190°C) for about 5 min..

Pat the fish fillets dry with paper towels. In a food processor, pulse the fish fillets until finely chopped but not pasty. Combine the chopped fish, Parmesan, onions, garlic, egg, salt, black pepper, and paprika in a large bowl. Mix well until all ingredients are evenly combined. Divide the mixture into 8 equal portions and shape each into a 1-inch thick patty. Brush the air fryer basket with olive oil to prevent sticking.

Place the fishcakes in the air fryer basket in a single layer, ensuring they do not touch each other. Cook for 10 min., then flip and cook for another 10 min. until golden brown and cooked through.

Nutritional Information (Approximate per serving):
Calories: 250, Protein: 25g, Fat: 15g, Carbs: 5g

62. Lobster in Butter Sauce

🍴 Servings: 4   🍲 Preparation Time: 10 min.   ⭕ Cooking Time: 15 min.

INGREDIENTS

- 4 lobster tails
- 1/2 cup unsalted butter, melted
- 2 cloves garlic, minced
- 1 tbsp lemon juice
- 1 tsp salt
- 1/2 tsp black pepper

DIRECTIONS:

Preheat your air fryer to 380°F (190°C) for about 5 min..

Cut the top shell of the lobster tails lengthwise down the middle using kitchen shears. Carefully pull the lobster meat out of the shell and place it on top of the shell for easy access and even cooking. Combine the butter, garlic, lemon juice, salt, and black pepper in a small bowl. Brush the lobster meat generously with the butter mixture.

Place the lobster tails in the air fryer basket. Cook for 10-12 min. until the lobster meat is opaque and cooked through, basting with additional butter sauce halfway through cooking.

Nutritional Information (Approximate per serving):
Calories: 250, Protein: 25g, Fat: 15g, Carbs: 1g

63. Octopus

🍴 Servings: 4   🍲 Preparation Time: 20 min.   ⭕ Cooking Time: 45 min.

INGREDIENTS

- 2 lbs octopus, cleaned
- 2 tbsp olive oil
- 1 tsp salt, smoked paprika
- 1/2 tsp black pepper
- 1 lemon, juiced
- 2 cloves garlic, minced
- 1/4 cup fresh parsley, chopped

DIRECTIONS:

Preheat your air fryer to 375°F (190°C) for about 5 min.

Rinse the octopus under cold water and pat dry with paper towels. Rub the octopus with olive oil, salt, black pepper, and smoked paprika.

Place the octopus in the air fryer basket. Cook for 40-45 min., flipping halfway through, until the octopus is tender and slightly crispy on the edges. Combine the lemon juice, garlic, and parsley in a small bowl. Remove the octopus from the air fryer and cut into bite-sized pieces.

Drizzle with the garlic lemon sauce. Serve hot, garnished with additional parsley and lemon wedges if desired.

Nutritional Information (Approximate per serving):
Calories: 250, Protein: 40g, Fat: 10g, Carbs: 2g

64. Crab Stuffed Squid

🍴 Servings: 4   🍲 Preparation Time: 20 min.   ⏲ Cooking Time: 15 min.

INGREDIENTS

- 8 medium-sized squid, cleaned
- 1/2 lb crab meat, cooked and shredded
- 1/4 cup grated Parmesan cheese
- 2 tbsp mayonnaise
- 2 cloves garlic, minced
- 1 tbsp lemon juice
- 1 tsp salt
- 1/2 tsp black pepper
- Olive oil spray
- Lemon wedges (optional for serving)

DIRECTIONS:

Preheat your air fryer to 375°F (190°C) for about 5 minutes.

Clean the squid thoroughly by removing the innards and the cartilage. Rinse under cold water and pat dry with paper towels.

Combine the shredded crab meat, grated Parmesan cheese, mayonnaise, minced garlic, lemon juice, salt, and black pepper in a large bowl. Mix well until all ingredients are evenly incorporated.

Carefully stuff each squid with the crab mixture using a small spoon. Be sure not to overfill to avoid bursting during cooking. Secure the open ends with toothpicks if necessary. Lightly spray the air fryer basket with olive oil spray.

Place the stuffed squid in the air fryer basket in a single layer. Lightly spray the tops of the squid with olive oil spray to help them crisp up.

Cook for 12-15 minutes, turning halfway through, until the squid is cooked through and slightly crispy on the outside.

Nutritional Information (Approximate per serving):
Calories: 250, Protein: 28g, Fat: 14g, Carbs: 4g

65. Squid in Sauce

Servings: 4   **Preparation Time:** 15 min.   **Cooking Time:** 20 min.

INGREDIENTS

- 1 lb squid, cleaned and cut into rings
- 2 tbsp olive oil
- 1 tsp salt
- 1/2 tsp black pepper
- 1 tsp garlic powder, smoked paprika
- 1/2 cup tomato sauce
- 1/4 cup heavy cream
- 2 cloves garlic, minced
- 1/4 cup fresh basil

DIRECTIONS:

Preheat your air fryer to 375°F (190°C) for about 5 min. Rinse the squid rings under cold water and pat dry with paper towels. Toss the squid rings with olive oil, salt, black pepper, garlic powder, and smoked paprika. Place the squid rings in the air fryer basket in a single layer. Cook for 10 min. shaking the basket halfway through. Heat the tomato sauce and garlic over medium heat in a small saucepan. Stir in the heavy cream and cook for 3-5 min. until the sauce is heated and slightly thickened. Stir in the chopped basil. Remove the squid rings from the air fryer and toss them in the tomato cream sauce. Serve hot, garnished with additional basil if desired.

Nutritional Information (Approximate per serving):
Calories: 300, Protein: 25g, Fat: 20g, Carbs: 5g

66. Cod with Pesto

Servings: 4   **Preparation Time:** 10 min.   **Cooking Time:** 12 min.

INGREDIENTS

- 4 cod fillets (about 6 oz each)
- 1/2 cup pesto sauce
- 2 tbsp olive oil
- 1 lemon, juiced
- 1 tsp salt
- 1/2 tsp black pepper
- 1/4 cup grated Parmesan

DIRECTIONS:

Preheat your air fryer to 390°F (200°C) for about 5 minutes.

Pat the cod fillets dry with paper towels. Rub each fillet with olive oil—season both sides with salt and black pepper. Place the cod fillets in the air fryer basket in a single layer. Cook for 10 min. until the fish is opaque and flakes easily with a fork. In a small bowl, combine the pesto sauce and lemon juice. Remove the cod fillets from the air fryer and place on serving plates.

Spoon the pesto sauce over the fillets and sprinkle with grated Parmesan.

Nutritional Information (Approximate per serving):
Calories: 350, Protein: 30g, Fat: 22g, Carbs: 2g

67. Seafood Stew

Servings: 4   **Preparation Time:** 20 min.   **Cooking Time:** 25 min.

INGREDIENTS

- 1/2 lb shrimp, peeled and deveined
- 1/2 lb scallops
- 1/2 lb cod fillet, cut into bite-sized pieces
- 1/2 lb mussels, cleaned
- 2 tbsp olive oil
- 1 small onion, finely chopped
- 2 cloves garlic, minced
- 1 cup fish broth or chicken broth
- 1/2 cup heavy cream
- 1 tsp salt
- 1/2 tsp black pepper
- 1 tsp smoked paprika
- 1/2 tsp dried thyme
- 1/2 tsp dried oregano
- Fresh parsley, chopped (optional, for garnish)

DIRECTIONS:

Preheat the air fryer to 375°F (190°C).

In an air fryer-safe dish, add the olive oil, chopped onions, and minced garlic. Cook for 5 minutes, stirring halfway through, until the onions are softened and fragrant.

Add the shrimp, scallops, cod, and mussels to the dish. Season with salt, pepper, smoked paprika, thyme, and oregano. Drizzle with olive oil and cook for 8-10 minutes until the seafood is just cooked through.

Once the seafood is cooked, pour in the fish (or chicken) broth and heavy cream.

Return the dish to the air fryer and cook at 350°F (175°C) for an additional 10 minutes, stirring occasionally, until the broth is heated through and the stew is slightly thickened.

Nutritional Information (Approximate per serving):
Calories: 350, Protein: 30g, Fat: 20g, Carbs: 8g

68. Smoked Crab

🍴 Servings: 4   🍲 Preparation Time: 10 min.   ⏲ Cooking Time: 15 min.

INGREDIENTS

- 2 lbs crab legs (king crab or snow crab)
- 1/4 cup melted butter
- 2 cloves garlic, minced
- 1 tbsp smoked paprika
- 1 tsp salt
- 1/2 tsp black pepper

DIRECTIONS:

Preheat your air fryer to 380°F (190°C) for about 5 minutes. Rinse the crab legs under cold water and pat dry with paper towels. Combine the melted butter, minced garlic, smoked paprika, salt, and black pepper in a small bowl. Brush the crab legs generously with the butter mixture.

Place the crab legs in the air fryer basket in a single layer. Cook for 10-12 min., until heated through, and the shells are slightly crispy.

Nutritional Information (Approximate per serving):
Calories: 300, Protein: 25g, Fat: 18g, Carbs: 1g

69. Oyster in Spicy Sauce

🍴 Servings: 4   🍲 Preparation Time: 15 min.   ⏲ Cooking Time: 10 min.

INGREDIENTS

- 24 fresh oysters, shucked
- 1/4 cup hot sauce (such as Sriracha or your favorite)
- 2 tbsp soy sauce (or coconut aminos for a soy-free option)
- 2 cloves garlic, minced
- 1 tbsp lemon juice, olive oil
- 1 tsp smoked paprika
- 1/2 tsp salt & black pepper

DIRECTIONS:

Preheat your air fryer to 400°F (200°C) for about 5 min.

Combine the hot sauce, soy sauce, minced garlic, lemon juice, olive oil, smoked paprika, salt, and black pepper in a small bowl. Mix well.

Shuck the oysters and place them on a tray or plate. Spoon a small amount of the spicy sauce over each oyster, ensuring they are well-coated.

Place the sauced oysters in the air fryer basket in a single layer. Cook for 8-10 min., until the oysters are cooked and slightly crispy on the edges.

Nutritional Information (Approximate per serving):
Calories: 200, Protein: 20g, Fat: 10g, Carbs: 3g

70. Shrimp in Cheese Sauce

Servings: 4 **Preparation Time:** 10 min. **Cooking Time:** 15 min.

INGREDIENTS

- 1 lb large shrimp, peeled and deveined
- 2 tbsp olive oil
- 1 tsp salt
- 1/2 tsp black pepper
- 1/2 tsp garlic powder
- 1/2 tsp paprika
- 1 cup heavy cream
- 1 cup grated cheddar cheese
- 1/4 cup grated Parmesan cheese
- 1 clove garlic, minced

DIRECTIONS:

Preheat the air fryer to 375°F (190°C).

Toss the shrimp with olive oil, salt, pepper, garlic powder, and paprika.

Place the shrimp in an air fryer-safe dish and cook for 8 minutes, shaking the basket halfway through, until the shrimp are pink and cooked through. Remove the shrimp from the air fryer and set aside.

In the same air fryer-safe dish, add the heavy cream, cheddar cheese, Parmesan cheese, and minced garlic. Cook in the air fryer at 350°F (175°C) for 4-5 minutes, stirring halfway through, until the cheese has melted and the sauce is creamy and smooth.

Return the cooked shrimp to the cheese sauce and stir to coat them evenly. Cook for an additional 1-2 minutes to heat everything through.

Nutritional Information (Approximate per serving):
Calories: 400, Protein: 30g, Fat: 30g, Carbs: 3g

71. Cheesy Crusted Salmon

Servings: 4 **Preparation Time:** 10 min. **Cooking Time:** 12 min.

INGREDIENTS

- 4 salmon fillets (about 6 oz each)
- 1/2 cup grated Parmesan, grated Mozzarella
- 2 tbsp olive oil
- 1 tsp garlic powder, onion powder, dried dill
- 1 lemon, juiced
- Salt and pepper

DIRECTIONS:

Preheat your air fryer to 390°F (200°C) for about 5 min. Pat the salmon fillets dry with paper towels. Rub each fillet with olive oil and lemon juice—season both sides with salt, black pepper, garlic powder, onion powder, and dried dill. Combine the parmesan, mozzarella cheese in a small bowl. Press the cheese mixture onto the top of each salmon fillet, ensuring they are well-coated.

Place the salmon fillets in the air fryer basket in a single layer. Cook for 10-12 min. until the cheese is melted and golden brown and the salmon is cooked and flakes easily with a fork.

Nutritional Information (Approximate per serving):
Calories: 450, Protein: 35g, Fat: 30g, Carbs: 3g

72. Ebi Tempura Shrimp

Servings: 4 **Preparation Time:** 20 min. **Cooking Time:** 10 min.

INGREDIENTS

- 1 lb large shrimp, peeled and deveined, tails on
- 1/2 cup sparkling water
- 1 large egg
- 1/2 tsp baking powder, salt
- 1/4 tsp black pepper, garlic powder, onion powder
- Cooking spray

DIRECTIONS:

Preheat your air fryer to 400°F (200°C) for about 5 min. In a medium bowl, whisk together the sparkling water, egg, baking powder, salt, black pepper, garlic powder, and onion powder until smooth. Pat the shrimp dry with paper towels. Dip each shrimp into the batter, allowing any excess to drip off. Lightly spray the air fryer basket with cooking spray. Place the battered shrimp in the air fryer basket in a single layer. Lightly spray the shrimp with cooking spray to help them crisp up. Cook for 5-6 min., flip the shrimp, and cook for another 4-5 min. until golden brown and crispy. Remove the shrimp from the air fryer and place on a serving platter.

Nutritional Information (Approximate per serving):
Calories: 300, Protein: 25g, Fat: 15g, Carbs: 10g

73. Mixed Seafood Kebabs

Servings: 4 **Preparation Time:** 10 min. **Cooking Time:** 10 min.

INGREDIENTS

- 8 oz white fish fillets (cut into chunks)
- 8 large shrimp, peeled and deveined
- 8 squid rings
- 1 tsp garlic powder
- 1/2 tsp salt, black pepper

DIRECTIONS:

Preheat the air fryer to 375°F (190°C), thread fish chunks, shrimp, and squid rings onto skewers, season with garlic powder, salt, and pepper, place in the air fryer basket, and cook for 8-10 minutes, turning halfway. Serve hot.

Nutritional Information (Approximate per serving):
Calories: 230, Protein: 32g, Fat: 10g, Carbs: 2g

74. King Prawn Scampi

Servings: 4 **Preparation Time:** 15 min. **Cooking Time:** 12 min.

INGREDIENTS

- 1 lb king prawns, peeled and deveined
- 2 large eggs, beaten
- 1 tsp salt
- 1/2 tsp black pepper, garlic powder, paprika
- Cooking spray
- Lemon wedges (optional for serving)

DIRECTIONS:

Pat the king prawns dry with paper towels. Dip each prawn into the beaten eggs, allowing any excess to drip off. Dredge the prawns in the Parmesan mixture, pressing lightly to adhere.

Lightly spray the air fryer basket with cooking spray. Place the breaded prawns in the air fryer basket in a single layer.

Lightly spray the prawns with cooking spray to help them crisp up. Cook for 5-6 min., then flip and cook for another 4-5 min. until golden brown and crispy.

Nutritional Information (Approximate per serving):
Calories: 350, Protein: 30g, Fat: 20g, Carbs: 6g

75. Cream Cheese Salmon Tempura

Servings: 4 **Preparation Time:** 20 min. **Cooking Time:** 12 min.

INGREDIENTS

- 1 lb salmon fillet, skin removed, cut into 1-inch strips
- 1/2 cup cream cheese, softened
- 1/4 cup green onions, finely chopped
- 1/2 cup sparkling water
- 1 large egg
- 1/2 tsp baking powder
- 1/2 tsp salt
- 1/4 tsp black pepper
- 1/4 tsp garlic powder
- 1/4 tsp onion powder
- Cooking spray

DIRECTIONS:

Preheat your air fryer to 400°F (200°C) for about 5 minutes.

Mix the softened cream cheese with the finely chopped green onions in a small bowl until well combined. Pat the salmon strips dry with paper towels. Using a small knife, make a slit in the center of each salmon strip to create a pocket. Fill each pocket with the cream cheese mixture.

In a medium bowl, whisk together the sparkling water, egg, baking powder, salt, black pepper, garlic powder, and onion powder until smooth. Dip each stuffed salmon strip into the batter, ensuring it is well coated. Lightly spray the air fryer basket with cooking spray.

Place the battered salmon strips in the air fryer basket in a single layer. Lightly spray the salmon strips with cooking spray to help them crisp up.

Cook for 5-6 minutes, then flip and cook for 4-5 minutes until golden brown and crispy.

Nutritional Information (Approximate per serving):
Calories: 400, Protein: 25g, Fat: 30g, Carbs: 5g

76. Panko Crusted Langoustines

Servings: 4 **Preparation Time:** 15 min. **Cooking Time:** 12 min.

INGREDIENTS

- 1 lb langoustines, peeled and deveined
- 1 cup panko breadcrumbs
- 1/2 cup grated Parmesan
- 2 large eggs, beaten
- 1 tsp salt
- 1/2 tsp black pepper, garlic powder, paprika
- garlic powder, onion powder, paprika

DIRECTIONS:

Preheat your air fryer to 390°F (200°C) for about 5 min. Combine the panko breadcrumbs, grated Parmesan, salt, black pepper, garlic powder, and paprika in a shallow dish. In another shallow dish, beat the eggs. Pat the langoustines dry with paper towels. Dip each langoustine into the beaten eggs, allowing any excess to drip off. Dredge the langoustines in the panko mixture, pressing lightly to adhere. Lightly spray the air fryer basket with cooking spray. Place the breaded langoustines in the air fryer basket in a single layer. Lightly spray the langoustines with cooking spray to help them crisp up. Cook for 5-6 min., then flip and cook for 4-5 min. until golden brown and crispy.

Nutritional Information (Approximate per serving):
Calories: 350, Protein: 30g, Fat: 20g, Carbs: 10g

77. Scallops in Sour Cream Sauce

Servings: 4 **Preparation Time:** 10 min. **Cooking Time:** 10 min.

INGREDIENTS

- 1 lb sea scallops
- 2 tbsp olive oil
- 1/2 tsp salt, black pepper, garlic powder
- 1/2 cup sour cream
- 1/4 cup grated Parmesan
- 2 tbsp fresh dill, chopped
- 1 tbsp lemon juice

DIRECTIONS:

Preheat your air fryer to 400°F (200°C) for about 5 min.

Pat the scallops dry with paper towels. Toss the scallops with olive oil, salt, black pepper, and garlic powder. Place the scallops in the air fryer basket in a single layer. Cook for 8-10 min, flipping halfway through, until the scallops are golden brown and cooked. Mix the sour cream, Parmesan, chopped dill, and lemon juice in a small bowl.

Remove the scallops from the air fryer and place on a serving platter. Spoon the sour cream sauce over the scallops.

Nutritional Information (Approximate per serving):
Calories: 300, Protein: 25g, Fat: 20g, Carbs: 3g

78. Herbed Baked Pollock

Servings: 4   **Preparation Time:** 10 min.   **Cooking Time:** 15 min.

INGREDIENTS

- 4 pollock fillets (about 6 oz each)
- 2 tbsp olive oil
- 1 tbsp lemon juice
- 2 cloves garlic, minced
- 1 tsp dried thyme, dried oregano, dried basil
- 1/2 tsp salt & black pepper

DIRECTIONS:

Preheat your air fryer to 375°F (190°C) for about 5 min. Pat the pollock fillets dry with paper towels. Mix the olive oil, lemon juice, garlic, dried thyme, dried oregano, dried basil, salt, and black pepper in a small bowl. Brush the herb mixture evenly over both sides of the pollock fillets. Place the fillets in the air fryer basket in a single layer. Cook for 12-15 min. until the fish is opaque and flakes easily with a fork.

Remove the fillets from the air fryer and place on a serving platter.

Nutritional Information (Approximate per serving):
Calories: 200, Protein: 30g, Fat: 10g, Carbs: 2g

79. Mussels with Cheese

Servings: 4   **Preparation Time:** 15 min.   **Cooking Time:** 10 min.

INGREDIENTS

- 2 lbs mussels, cleaned and debearded
- 1/2 cup grated Parmesan
- 1/2 cup shredded Mozzarella
- 2 cloves garlic, minced
- 2 tbsp fresh parsley, chopped
- 1 tbsp olive oil

DIRECTIONS:

Preheat your air fryer to 400°F (200°C) for about 5 min. Rinse the mussels under cold water and scrub the shells. Discard any mussels that are open and do not close when tapped. Combine the parmesan, mozzarella, garlic, and parsley in a small bowl. Arrange the mussels in a single layer in the air fryer basket. Drizzle with olive oil and season with salt and pepper. Sprinkle the cheese mixture evenly over the mussels. Cook for 8-10 min., until the mussels open and the cheese is melted and bubbly.

Nutritional Information (Approximate per serving):
Calories: 250, Protein: 20g, Fat: 15g, Carbs: 5g

80. Battered Shrimp Cheese Balls

Servings: 4 **Preparation Time:** 20 min. **Cooking Time:** 10 min.

INGREDIENTS

- 1 lb large shrimp, peeled and deveined, finely chopped
- 1 cup shredded Mozzarella
- 1/2 cup grated Parmesan
- 1/2 cup sparkling water
- 1 large egg
- 1/2 tsp baking powder, salt
- 1/4 tsp black pepper, garlic powder, onion powder

DIRECTIONS:

Preheat your air fryer to 400°F (200°C) for about 5 min.

Combine the shrimp, mozzarella, and d Parmesan in a large bowl. Mix well. Form the mixture into 16 small balls, about 1 inch in diameter. In a medium bowl, whisk together the sparkling water, egg, baking powder, salt, black pepper, garlic powder, and onion powder until smooth. Dip each shrimp cheese ball into the batter, allowing any excess to drip off. Lightly spray the air fryer basket with cooking spray.

Place the battered shrimp cheese balls in the air fryer basket in a single layer. Lightly spray the shrimp cheese balls with cooking spray to help them crisp up. Cook for 8-10 min., until golden brown and crispy.

Nutritional Information (Approximate per serving):
Calories: 400, Protein: 30g, Fat: 25g, Carbs: 5g

CHAPTER 12

ORGAN MEATS

81. Beef Heart Skewers 80
82. Chicken Pate 80
83. Braised Turkey Gizzards 81
84. Poached Beef Tongue with Gravy 81
85. Battered Pork Kidneys with Soy Sauce 82

86. Chicken Offal 82
87. Bacon Pate 83
88. Veal Heart Roast 83
89. Chicken Gizzard Roast 84
90. Liver Pancakes 84

81. Beef Heart Skewers

Servings: 4   Preparation Time: 15 min.   Cooking Time: 20 min.

INGREDIENTS

- 1 lb beef heart, trimmed and cut into cubes
- 2 tbsp olive oil
- 1 tsp salt
- 1/2 tsp black pepper
- 1 tsp garlic powder, smoked paprika
- Wooden skewers, soaked in water for 30 min.

DIRECTIONS:

Preheat your air fryer to 375°F (190°C) for about 5 min.

Toss the beef heart cubes with olive oil, salt, black pepper, garlic powder, and smoked paprika. Thread the beef heart cubes onto the soaked wooden skewers.

Place the skewers in the air fryer basket in a single layer. Cook for 10 min., then flip and cook for another 10 min. until the beef heart is cooked and slightly charred on the edges.

Nutritional Information (Approximate per serving):
Calories: 220, Protein: 28g, Fat: 12g, Carbs: 1g

82. Chicken Pate

Servings: 4   Preparation Time: 15 min.   Cooking Time: 20 min.

INGREDIENTS

- 1 lb chicken livers, cleaned and trimmed
- 1 small onion, finely chopped
- 2 cloves garlic, minced
- 1/4 cup heavy cream
- 4 tbsp unsalted butter, divided
- 2 tbsp olive oil
- 1 tsp salt
- 1/2 tsp black pepper, dried thyme

DIRECTIONS:

Preheat the air fryer to 375°F (190°C). Add 2 tbsp of butter, olive oil, onions, and garlic in an air fryer-safe dish. Cook for 5 min., stirring halfway through, until the onions are soft and translucent. Add the cleaned and trimmed chicken livers to the same dish—season with salt, pepper, and dried thyme. Cook for 10-12 min., stirring halfway through, until the livers are cooked but still slightly pink inside.

Once cooked, transfer the livers and onions to a food processor or blender. Add the heavy cream and the remaining 2 tbsp of butter. Blend until smooth and creamy. Taste and adjust seasoning if needed. Allow the pâté to cool slightly, then refrigerate for at least an hour to allow the flavors to meld.

Nutritional Information (Approximate per serving):
Calories: 300, Protein: 25g, Fat: 22g, Carbs: 3g

83. Braised Turkey Gizzards

Servings: 4 **Preparation Time:** 15 min. **Cooking Time:** 40 min.

INGREDIENTS

- 1 lb turkey gizzards, cleaned
- 1 small onion, finely chopped
- 2 cloves garlic, minced
- 2 cups chicken broth
- 2 tbsp olive oil
- 1 tsp salt, 1/2 tsp black pepper
- 1 tsp smoked paprika, dried thyme

DIRECTIONS:

Preheat the air fryer to 375°F (190°C).

Add olive oil, onion, and garlic in an air fryer-safe dish. Cook for 5 min., stirring halfway through, until the onions are soft and fragrant. Add the cleaned turkey gizzards to the dish and season with salt, black pepper, smoked paprika, and dried thyme. Cook for 10 min. to brown the gizzards, stirring halfway through.

After browning, pour the chicken broth over the gizzards.

Reduce the air fryer temperature to 350°F (175°C) and cook for 25 min., stirring occasionally, until the gizzards are tender and the broth has reduced slightly.

Nutritional Information (Approximate per serving):
Calories: 250, Protein: 28g, Fat: 12g, Carbs: 3g

84. Poached Beef Tongue with Gravy

Servings: 4 **Preparation Time:** 20 min. **Cooking Time:** 60 min.

INGREDIENTS

- 1 lb beef tongue, cleaned
- 4 cups beef broth
- 1 small onion, chopped
- 2 cloves garlic, minced
- 2 bay leaves
- 1 tsp salt, 1/2 tsp black pepper
- 2 tbsp olive oil, pork rinds

DIRECTIONS:

Preheat the air fryer to 375°F (190°C).

In an air fryer-safe dish, add the cleaned beef tongue, beef broth, onion, garlic, bay leaves, salt, and black pepper. Cook for 45 min., flipping the tongue halfway through and stirring occasionally to ensure even cooking. After 45 min., remove the beef tongue and set it aside to cool slightly. Once cooled, peel the skin off the tongue and slice it thinly. To prepare the gravy, add the heavy cream and crushed pork rinds to the remaining broth in the air fryer-safe dish. Cook in the air fryer at 350°F (175°C) for another 10 min., stirring occasionally, until the sauce thickens to a gravy-like consistency.

Nutritional Information (Approximate per serving):
Calories: 350, Protein: 30g, Fat: 22g, Carbs: 4g

85. Battered Pork Kidneys with Soy Sauce

Servings: 4 **Preparation Time:** 20 min. **Cooking Time:** 17 min.

INGREDIENTS

- 1 lb pork kidneys, cleaned and cut into bite-sized pieces
- 2 large eggs, beaten
- 1/2 cup panko breadcrumbs
- 2 tbsp soy sauce (or coconut aminos)
- 1 tbsp olive oil
- 1 tsp salt
- 1/2 tsp black pepper
- 1/2 tsp garlic powder
- Cooking spray
- Fresh cilantro, chopped

DIRECTIONS:

Preheat the air fryer to 375°F (190°C).

In a bowl, season the cleaned and cut pork kidneys with salt, pepper, and garlic powder. In a separate bowl, beat the eggs, and in another bowl, place the panko breadcrumbs.

Dip each piece of kidney into the beaten eggs, then coat with the panko breadcrumbs. Lightly spray or brush the air fryer basket with olive oil to prevent sticking.

Place the breaded kidneys in the basket in a single layer. Cook for 12-15 min., flipping halfway through, until golden brown and crispy. In a small bowl, mix the soy sauce with 1 tbsp of olive oil. Drizzle the soy sauce mixture over the cooked kidneys or serve it on the side as a dipping sauce.

Nutritional Information (Approximate per serving):
Calories: 300, Protein: 28g, Fat: 18g, Carbs: 5g

86. Chicken Offal

Servings: 4 **Preparation Time:** 10 min. **Cooking Time:** 20 min.

INGREDIENTS

- 1 lb chicken offal (hearts, livers, gizzards), cleaned and trimmed
- 2 tbsp olive oil
- 1 tsp salt
- 1/2 tsp black pepper
- 1 tsp garlic powder, smoked paprika

DIRECTIONS:

Preheat your air fryer to 400°F (200°C) for about 5 min.

Toss the chicken offal with olive oil, salt, black pepper, garlic powder, and smoked paprika until well coated.

Place the chicken offal in the air fryer basket in a single layer. Cook for 10 min, shaking the basket halfway through or until the refuse is browned and cooked through.

Nutritional Information (Approximate per serving):
Calories: 220, Protein: 25g, Fat: 12g, Carbs: 2g

87. Bacon Pate

🍴 Servings: 4   🍲 Preparation Time: 15 min.   ⭕ Cooking Time: 20 min

INGREDIENTS

- 1 lb chicken livers, cleaned and trimmed
- 6 slices bacon, chopped
- 1 small onion, finely chopped
- 2 cloves garlic, minced
- 1/4 cup heavy cream
- 4 tbsp unsalted butter, divided
- 1 tsp salt, 1/2 tsp black pepper&thyme

DIRECTIONS:

Preheat the air fryer to 375°F (190°C).

In an air fryer-safe dish, cook the bacon for 5-6 min. until crispy. Remove the bacon and set aside, leaving the rendered fat in the dish. Add 2 tbsp of butter, the chopped onion, and minced garlic to the same dish. Cook for 5 min., stirring halfway through, until the onions are soft and fragrant. Next, add the cleaned chicken livers, salt, pepper, and thyme to the dish. Cook for 10-12 min., stirring occasionally, until the livers are fully cooked but still slightly pink in the center. Remove from the air fryer and let cool slightly.

Transfer the cooked chicken livers, bacon, the remaining 2 tbsp of butter, and the heavy cream to a food processor or blender. Blend until smooth and creamy.

Nutritional Information (Approximate per serving):
Calories: 350, Protein: 30g, Fat: 24g, Carbs: 3g

88. Veal Heart Roast

🍴 Servings: 4   🍲 Preparation Time: 20 min.   ⭕ Cooking Time: 1 hour.

INGREDIENTS

- 1 lb veal heart, cleaned and trimmed
- 2 tbsp olive oil
- 1 tsp salt, 1/2 tsp black pepper
- 1 tsp garlic powder, dried rosemary, dried thyme

DIRECTIONS:

Preheat your air fryer to 350°F (175°C) for about 5 min. Rinse the veal heart under cold water and pat dry with paper towels. Rub the veal heart with olive oil, salt, black pepper, garlic powder, rosemary, and thyme.

Place the veal heart in the air fryer basket. Cook for 30 min., flip the heat, and cook for another 30 min. until the internal temperature reaches 145°F (63°C).

Nutritional Information (Approximate per serving):
Calories: 300, Protein: 40g, Fat: 15g, Carbs: 1g

89. Chicken Gizzard Roast

Servings: 4   **Preparation Time:** 15 min.   **Cooking Time:** 35 min.

INGREDIENTS

- 1 lb chicken gizzards, cleaned
- 2 tbsp olive oil
- 1 tsp salt, 1/2 tsp black pepper
- 1 tsp garlic powder, paprika

DIRECTIONS:

Preheat your air fryer to 375°F (190°C) for about 5 min.

Toss the chicken gizzards with olive oil, salt, black pepper, garlic powder, and paprika until well coated.

Place the gizzards in the air fryer basket in a single layer. Cook for 20 min., shaking the basket halfway through. Cook for 15 min. or until the gizzards are tender and slightly crispy.

Nutritional Information (Approximate per serving):
Calories: 250, Protein: 28g, Fat: 12g, Carbs: 2g

90. Liver Pancakes

Servings: 4   **Preparation Time:** 15 min.   **Cooking Time:** 20 min.

INGREDIENTS

- 1 lb chicken livers, cleaned and trimmed
- 1 small onion, finely chopped
- 2 cloves garlic, minced
- 2 large eggs
- 1/4 cup heavy cream
- 1 tsp salt
- 1/2 tsp black pepper, garlic powder, onion powder
- 2 tbsp olive oil

DIRECTIONS:

Preheat your air fryer to 375°F (190°C) for about 5 min..

In a food processor, combine the chicken livers, onion, minced garlic, eggs, heavy cream, salt, black pepper, garlic powder, and onion powder. Blend until smooth and well combined. Lightly spray a parchment paper or silicone mat with cooking spray.

Spoon the liver mixture onto the parchment paper or mat, forming small pancakes about 3-4 inches in diameter. Drizzle the pancakes with olive oil to help them crisp up.

Place the parchment paper or silicone mat in the air fryer basket with the pancakes. Cook for 10 min., then carefully flip the pancakes and cook for another 10 min. until they are firm and slightly crispy on the edges.

Nutritional Information (Approximate per serving):
Calories: 300, Protein: 25g, Fat: 20g, Carbs: 3g

CHAPTER 13

SNACKS & APPETIZERS

91. Chicken Wings 86
92. Pork Rinds 86
93. Deviled Eggs... 87
94. Sausage Bites 87
95. Mozzarella Sticks 88

96. Cheese Crisps.. 88
97. Flavorful Air Fryer Jerky 89
98. Beef Liver Chips.. 89
99. Ham Croquettes 90
100. Glazed Shrimp Skewers 90

91. Chicken Wings

Servings: 4 **Preparation Time:** 10 min. **Cooking Time:** 25 min.

INGREDIENTS

- 2 lbs chicken wings
- 2 tbsp olive oil
- 1 tsp salt, 1/2 tsp black pepper
- 1 tsp garlic powder, paprika

DIRECTIONS:

Preheat your air fryer to 400°F (200°C) for about 5 min..

Toss the chicken wings with olive oil, salt, black pepper, garlic powder, and paprika until well coated.

Place the wings in the air fryer basket in a single layer. Cook for 25 min., shaking the basket halfway through, until the wings are crispy and cooked.

Nutritional Information (Approximate per serving):
Calories: 350, Protein: 25g, Fat: 25g, Carbs: 1g

92. Pork Rinds

Servings: 4 **Preparation Time:** 5 min. **Cooking Time:** 15 min.

INGREDIENTS

- 1 lb pork skin, cut into bite-sized pieces
- 1 tsp salt
- 1/2 tsp paprika (optional)

DIRECTIONS:

Preheat your air fryer to 390°F (200°C) for about 5 min.

Pat the pork skin dry with paper towels. Season with salt and paprika if using.

Place the pork skin pieces in the air fryer basket in a single layer. Cook for 15 min., shaking the basket every 5 min. until crispy and puffed up..

Nutritional Information (Approximate per serving):
Calories: 150, Protein: 12g, Fat: 10g, Carbs: 0g

93. Deviled Eggs

Servings: 4 **Preparation Time:** 15 min. **Cooking Time:** 15 min.

INGREDIENTS

- 8 large eggs
- 1/4 cup mayonnaise
- 1 tbsp Dijon mustard
- 1 tsp apple cider vinegar
- 1/4 tsp salt & pepper
- Paprika for garnish

DIRECTIONS:

Preheat your air fryer to 270°F (130°C).

Place the eggs in the air fryer basket and cook for 15 min.. Immediately transfer the eggs to an ice bath to cool, then peel. Halve the eggs and remove the yolks.

Mash the yolks with mayonnaise, Dijon mustard, apple cider vinegar, salt, and black pepper until smooth. Spoon or pipe the yolk mixture back into the egg whites.

Garnish with a sprinkle of paprika. Arrange on a serving platter and serve chilled.

Nutritional Information (Approximate per serving):
Calories: 150, Protein: 12g, Fat: 12g, Carbs: 1g

94. Sausage Bites

Servings: 4 **Preparation Time:** 10 min. **Cooking Time:** 10 min.

INGREDIENTS

- 1 lb sausage links
- 1 tbsp olive oil
- 1 tsp salt
- 1/2 tsp black pepper

DIRECTIONS:

Preheat your air fryer to 400°F (200°C) for about 5 min. Cut the sausage links into bite-sized pieces. Toss with olive oil, salt, and black pepper.

Place the sausage bites in the air fryer basket in a single layer. Cook for 10 min., shaking the basket halfway through, until browned and cooked.

Nutritional Information (Approximate per serving):
Calories: 250, Protein: 20g, Fat: 18g, Carbs: 1g

95. Mozzarella Sticks

Servings: 4 **Preparation Time:** 75 min. **Cooking Time:** 10 min.

INGREDIENTS

- 8 mozzarella sticks
- 2 large eggs, beaten
- 1/2 cup grated Parmesan
- 1 tsp Italian seasoning

DIRECTIONS:

Preheat your air fryer to 400°F (200°C).

In a shallow dish, mix the parmesan and Italian seasoning. In another shallow dish, beat the eggs. Dredge each mozzarella stick in the parmesan mixture, dip in the beaten eggs, and coat again with the Parmesan cheese mixture. Ensure each stick is fully covered.

Place the coated sticks on a tray and freeze for at least 1 hour to prevent the cheese from melting too quickly during cooking. Lightly spray the air fryer basket with cooking spray. Place the frozen mozzarella sticks in the air fryer basket in a single layer. Cook for 8-10 min., until golden and crispy.

Nutritional Information (Approximate per serving):
Calories: 250, Protein: 20g, Fat: 18g, Carbs: 2g

96. Cheese Crisps

Servings: 4 **Preparation Time:** 5 min. **Freeze Time:** 8 min.

INGREDIENTS

- 1 cup shredded cheddar
- 1/2 cup grated Parmesan
- 1/2 tsp garlic powder

DIRECTIONS:

Preheat the air fryer to 350°F (175°C).

Mix the shredded cheddar, parmesan, and garlic powder together. Scoop small mounds of the cheese mixture onto a parchment-lined air fryer basket, leaving space between each.

Cook for 6-8 min. until the cheese has melted and turned golden brown and crispy. Allow the crisps to cool and harden before serving.

Nutritional Information (Approximate per serving):
Calories: 220, Protein: 15g, Fat: 18g, Carbs: 1g

97. Flavorful Jerky

Servings: 4   **Preparation Time:** 4 hours 15 min   **Chill Time:** 2 hours.

INGREDIENTS

- 1 lb game meat (venison, elk, or bison), thinly sliced
- 1/4 cup soy sauce
- 1/4 cup Worcestershire sauce
- 2 tbsp apple cider vinegar, olive oil
- 1 tbsp honey
- 2 cloves garlic, minced, 1/2 tsp onion powder
- 1 tsp smoked paprika, pepper

DIRECTIONS:

Whisk together the soy sauce, Worcestershire sauce, apple cider vinegar, olive oil, honey, minced garlic, smoked paprika, black pepper, and onion powder in a bowl.

Place the sliced game meat in a resealable plastic bag and pour the marinade over it. Seal the bag and massage the marinade into the meat. Refrigerate for at least 4 hours or overnight for best results.

Preheat your air fryer to 160°F (70°C) for about 5 min.

Remove the meat from the marinade and pat dry with paper towels. Arrange the meat slices in a single layer in the air fryer basket.

Cook for 2 hours, flipping the meat halfway through, until the jerky is dry and slightly chewy. Remove the jerky from the air fryer and let it cool completely before serving.

Nutritional Information (Approximate per serving):
Calories: 150, Protein: 25g, Fat: 4g, Carbs: 3g

98. Beef Liver Chips

Servings: 4   **Preparation Time:** 10 min.   **Cooking Time:** 15 min.

INGREDIENTS

- 1 lb beef liver, thinly sliced
- 2 tbsp olive oil
- 1 tsp salt
- 1/2 tsp black pepper

DIRECTIONS:

Preheat the air fryer to 375°F (190°C).

Toss the thinly sliced beef liver in olive oil, salt, and pepper. Lay the slices in a single layer in the air fryer basket.

Cook for 10-15 min., flipping halfway through, until crispy and golden brown.

Nutritional Information (Approximate per serving):
Calories: 180, Protein: 25g, Fat: 8g, Carbs: 1g

99. Ham Croquettes

Servings: 4 **Preparation Time: 20 min.** **Freeze Time: 12 min.**

INGREDIENTS

- 2 cups cooked ham, finely chopped
- 1/2 cup shredded cheddar
- 1/4 cup heavy cream, grated Parmesan
- 2 large eggs, beaten
- 1 tsp garlic powder, onion powder
- 1/2 tsp salt & pepper

DIRECTIONS:

Preheat your air fryer to 375°F (190°C). Combine the ham, shredded cheddar, heavy cream, parmesan, beaten eggs, garlic powder, onion powder, salt, and black pepper in a large bowl. Mix well until all ingredients are thoroughly combined. Shape the mixture into small oval-shaped croquettes using your hands. Lightly spray the air fryer basket with cooking spray. Place the croquettes in the air fryer basket in a single layer. Lightly spray the croquettes with cooking spray to help them crisp up. Cook for 10-12 min., turning halfway through, until golden brown and crispy.

Nutritional Information (Approximate per serving):
Calories: 300, Protein: 20g, Fat: 22g, Carbs: 4g

100. Glazed Shrimp Skewers

Servings: 4 **Preparation Time: 15 min.** **Cooking Time: 10 min.**

INGREDIENTS

- 1 lb large shrimp, peeled and deveined
- 2 tbsp olive oil, honey
- 2 tbsp soy sauce
- 1 tbsp lime juice
- 1 clove garlic, minced
- 1/2 tsp red pepper flakes
- Wooden skewers, soaked in water for 30 minutes

DIRECTIONS:

Preheat your air fryer to 400°F (200°C).

Whisk together the olive oil, honey, soy sauce, lime juice, garlic, and red pepper flakes in a bowl. Toss the shrimp in the marinade and let it sit for 10-15 min.. Thread the marinated shrimp onto the soaked wooden skewers.

Place the shrimp skewers in the air fryer basket in a single layer. Cook for 8-10 min., turning halfway through, until the shrimp are pink and opaque.

Nutritional Information (Approximate per serving):
Calories: 200, Protein: 25g, Fat: 8g, Carbs: 10g

CHAPTER 14:
TOP 10 QUESTIONS AND ANSWERS ABOUT THE CARNIVORE

1. What is the carnivore diet?

The carnivore diet, or all-meat, involves consuming only animal-based foods such as meat, fish, eggs, and some dairy products. It excludes all plant-based foods, including fruits, vegetables, grains, nuts, and seeds. Proponents of this diet believe it can lead to numerous health benefits, including weight loss, improved digestion, and increased energy levels.

2. Why do people choose the carnivore diet?

People choose the carnivore diet for various reasons, including weight loss, autoimmune disease management, mental clarity, and overall health improvement. Many individuals report feeling better, experiencing fewer digestive issues, and having more stable energy levels on this diet.

3. Is the carnivore diet safe?

The safety of the carnivore diet can vary depending on the individual. Some people thrive on a meat-based diet, while others may experience deficiencies or health issues. It's essential to consult with a healthcare professional before starting any restrictive diet, especially if you have underlying health conditions or are on medication.

4. What are the potential benefits of the carnivore diet?

Potential benefits of the carnivore diet include weight loss, improved mental clarity, reduced inflammation, and better digestion. Many also report enhanced energy levels and reduced chronic pain and autoimmune symptoms.

5. What are the possible drawbacks of the carnivore diet?

Possible drawbacks include nutrient deficiencies, particularly in vitamins C and E, fiber, and certain minerals in plant-based foods. Additionally, the diet can be socially restrictive and may lead to increased cholesterol levels in some individuals.

Cooking: Preheat your air fryer to 400°F—season with salt and pepper. Cook for 15-18 minutes, flipping halfway through, until the internal temperature reaches 135°F for medium-rare. Let it rest for a few minutes before serving.

6. How do I start the carnivore diet?

To start the carnivore diet, gradually eliminate plant-based foods, focusing on consuming high-quality meats, fish, eggs, and dairy products. It's also helpful to plan meals and snacks to ensure you have a variety of foods available and to avoid cravings for non-carnivore foods.

7. Can I get all the necessary nutrients from the carnivore diet?
While the carnivore diet provides many essential nutrients, obtaining specific vitamins and minerals from animal products can be challenging. Supplements may be necessary for vitamin C, fiber, and magnesium. Consulting with a healthcare professional or a dietitian can help address potential deficiencies.

8. Is the carnivore diet sustainable long-term?
The long-term sustainability of the carnivore diet depends on the individual's health goals, preferences, and how their body responds to the diet. Some people maintain the diet for years with positive results, while others may find it too restrictive or encounter health issues that necessitate a more balanced approach.

9. What are some common challenges on the carnivore diet?
Common challenges include social situations where non-carnivore foods are served, cravings for plant-based foods, potential nutrient deficiencies, and the cost of high-quality meats and animal products. Planning and finding a supportive community can help overcome these obstacles.

10. How can I ensure variety and enjoyment in my meals on the carnivore diet?
To ensure variety and enjoyment, experiment with different cuts of meat, cooking methods, and animal-based ingredients. An air fryer can help create delicious, crispy textures and make meal preparation easier. Incorporating spices, herbs, and different cooking techniques can keep your meals exciting and satisfying.

42-DAY MEAL PLAN

WEEK ___1___

	BREAKFAST	LUNCH	DINNER
MON	Bacon and Eggs	Pork Chops with Herb Crust	Salmon in Sour Cream Sauce
TUE	Pork Sausage	Rack of Lamb	Beef Heart Skewers
WED	Beef Steak and Eggs	Meatloaf	Fish cakes
THU	Ham and Egg Cups	Lamb Kebab	Lobster in Butter Sauce
FRI	Breakfast Meatballs	Glazed Ribs	Chicken Pate
SAT	Chicken Sausages	Carnivore Burger	Crab Stuffed Squid
SUN	Scotch Eggs	Ground Pork Frittata	Octopus

WEEK ___2___

	BREAKFAST	LUNCH	DINNER
MON	Scotch Eggs	Braised Rabbit Pie	Squid in Sauce
TUE	Beef Liver and Egg Scramble	Ribeye Steak	Seafood Stew
WED	Pork Breakfast Tacos	T-Bone Steak	Braised Turkey Gizzards
THU	Shrimp and Egg Scramble	Filet Mignon	Cod with Pesto
FRI	Cod and Egg Breakfast Bowls	New York Strip Steak	Smoked Crab
SAT	Bacon and Steak Frittata	Bison Meatloaf	Poached Beef Tongue with Gravy
SUN	Ham and Cheese Breakfast Rolls	Lamb and Feta Patties	Oyster in Spicy Sauce

WEEK 3

	BREAKFAST	LUNCH	DINNER
MON	Carnivore Breakfast Pizza	Bacon-Wrapped Pork Tenderloin	Shrimp in Cheese Sauce
TUE	Beef and Cheese Omelette	Escalope of Lamb	Battered Pork Kidneys with Soy Sauce
WED	Shrimp and Bacon Skewers	Whiskey Marinated Beef	Cheesy Crusted Salmon
THU	Chicken Heart and Egg Skewers	Breaded Pork Steak	Ebi Tempura Shrimp
FRI	Turkey Heart and Scallop Scramble	Beef Steaks in Hot Sauce	Chicken Offal
SAT	Bacon and Eggs	Bone-in Pork Cutlets	Battered Shrimp Cheese Balls
SUN	Pork Sausage	Beef with Egg Butter Sauce	Cream Cheese Salmon Tempura

WEEK 4

	BREAKFAST	LUNCH	DINNER
MON	Beef Steak and Eggs	Elk Steak	Panko Crusted Langoustines
TUE	Ham and Egg Cups	Seasoned Chicken Drumsticks	Bacon Pate
WED	Breakfast Meatballs	Seasoned Chicken Drumsticks	King Prawn Scampi
THU	Chicken Sausages	Turkey Breast	Mussels with Cheese
FRI	Scotch Eggs	Chicken Roulade	Veal Heart Roast
SAT	Bacon and Eggs	Smoked Chicken	Herbed Baked Pollock
SUN	Beef Liver and Egg Scramble	Turkey Bacon Medallions	Scallops in Sour Cream Sauce

WEEK 5

	BREAKFAST	LUNCH	DINNER
MON	Pork Breakfast Tacos	Turkey Cutlets Stuffed with Bacon and Cheese	Salmon in Sour Cream Sauce
TUE	Shrimp and Egg Scramble	Turkey Turrets	Chicken Gizzard Roast
WED	Cod and Egg Breakfast Bowls	Crispy Duck Breast	Fish cakes
THU	Bacon and Steak Frittata	Quail with Herb Butter	Lobster in Butter Sauce
FRI	Ham and Cheese Breakfast Rolls	Chicken Soufflé	Liver Pancakes
SAT	Bacon and Eggs	Turkey Muffins	Crab Stuffed Squid
SUN	Pork Sausage	Parmesan Baked Duck	Octopus

WEEK 6

	BREAKFAST	LUNCH	DINNER
MON	Scotch Eggs	Chicken Cutlets with Cottage Cheese	Squid in Sauce
TUE	Beef Liver and Egg Scramble	Turkey and Cheese Pie	Beef Heart Skewers
WED	Pork Breakfast Tacos	Smoked Turkey Legs	Cod with Pesto
THU	Shrimp and Egg Scramble	Chicken Legs Wrapped in Bacon	Smoked Crab
FRI	Cod and Egg Breakfast Bowls	Creamy Chicken Breast	Chicken Pate
SAT	Bacon and Steak Frittata	Turkey Bacon Medallions	Herbed Baked Pollock
SUN	Ham and Cheese Breakfast Rolls	Turkey Cutlets Stuffed with Bacon and Cheese	Air Fryer Scallops in Sour Cream Sauce

COOKING CONVERSION CHART

MEASUREMENT CONVERSIONS

VOLUME EQUIVALENTS (DRY):

US STANDART	METRIC (APPROXIMATE)
1/8 TEASPOON (TSP)	0,5 ML
1/4 TEASPOON (TSP)	1 ML
1/2 TEASPOON (TSP)	2 ML
3/4 TEASPOON (TSP)	4 ML
1 TEASPOON (TSP)	5 ML
1 TABLESPOON (TBSP)	15 ML
1/4 CUP	59 ML
1/3 CUP	79 ML
1/2 CUP	118 ML
2/3 CUP	156 ML
3/4 CUP	177 ML
1 CUP	235 ML
2 CUPS OR 1 PINT (PT)	473 ML
3 CUPS	700 ML
4 CUPS OR 1 QUART	1 L
1/2 GALLON	2 L
1 GALLON	4 L

WEIGHT EQUIVALENTS:

US STANDART	METRIC (APPROXIMATE)
1/2 OUNCE (OZ)	15 G
1 OUNCE (OZ)	30 G
2 OUNCE (OZ)	60 G
4 OUNCE (OZ)	115 G
8 OUNCE (OZ)	225 G
12 OUNCE (OZ)	340 G
16 OUNCE OR 1 POUND	455 G
2.2 POUNDS (LBS)	1 kilogram (kg)

VOLUME EQUIVALENTS (LIQUID):

US STANDART	US STANDART (OUNCES)	METRIC (APPROXIMATE)
2 TABLESPOONS	1 FL.OZ.	30 ML
1/4 CUP	2 FL.OZ.	60 ML
1/2 CUP	4 FL.OZ.	120 ML
1 CUP	8 FL.OZ.	240 ML
2 CUPS OR 1 PINT	16 FL.OZ.	475 ML
4 CUPS OR 1 QUART	32 FL.OZ.	1 L
1 GALLON	128 FL.OZ.	4 L

OVEN TEMPERATURES

FAHRENHEIT (F)	CELSIUS (C) (APPROXIMATE)
250°F	120°C
300°F	150°C
325°F	180°C
375°F	190°C
400°F	200°C
425°F	220°C

CONCLUSION

The Carnivore Diet Air Fryer cookbook" provides a wealth of delicious and nutritious recipes that are simple to prepare and tailored to the unique needs of a carnivore diet. By incorporating the air fryer into your culinary routine, you can enjoy a variety of flavorful meals that are crispy, tender, and cooked to perfection with minimal effort. This cookbook aims to make your journey on the carnivore diet enjoyable and sustainable, highlighting the versatility of meat-based dishes while maintaining convenience and health.

A carnivore diet can bring numerous health benefits, including weight loss, improved digestion, and enhanced mental clarity. The recipes in this book are designed to support these benefits by focusing on high-quality animal products that provide essential nutrients and promote overall well-being. Each recipe has been crafted from breakfast to dinner, snacks, and appetizers to ensure a diverse and satisfying eating experience.

One key advantage of using an air fryer is its ability to create healthier versions of traditionally fried foods. By reducing the amount of oil needed for cooking, the air fryer helps you maintain a diet low in unhealthy fats while still delivering deliciously crispy textures. This cooking method also saves time and energy, making sticking to your dietary goals easier.

The carnivore diet may come with challenges, but proper planning and the right tools can be a rewarding and enjoyable lifestyle. This cookbook has equipped you with practical tips and mouth-watering recipes that make adhering to your dietary preferences easier without feeling deprived. You can keep your meals exciting and nutritious by exploring different cuts of meat, experimenting with spices, and utilizing various cooking techniques.

As you continue your carnivore journey, remember that your body is unique and your diet should reflect that. Everyone's nutritional requirements are different, and it's crucial to ensure you're getting all the essential nutrients for optimal health. Consider consulting with a healthcare professional or a nutritionist to tailor the diet to your specific needs. This way, you can confidently navigate your carnivore diet, knowing that it's designed with you in mind.

We hope this cookbook has inspired you to embrace the carnivore diet with enthusiasm and creativity. The air fryer is a powerful tool that can transform your meals and make the diet more accessible and enjoyable. These recipes allow you to enjoy various tasty, nutrient-dense meals that align with your dietary goals.

Thank you for choosing "The Carnivore Diet Air Fryer cookbook" as your guide. We wish you great success on your health journey and hope you continue discovering the joys of a meat-based diet. Happy cooking and bon appétit!

Printed in Great Britain
by Amazon